TEACHER RECOMMENDED

7th GRADE COMMON CORE MATH
DAILY PRACTICE WORKBOOK

PART I: MULTIPLE CHOICE

ARGOPREP.COM

FREE ONLINE SYSTEM WITH VIDEO EXPLANATIONS

ArgoPrep is one of the leading providers of supplemental educational products and services. We offer affordable and effective test prep solutions to educators, parents and students. Learning should be fun and easy! For that reason, most of our workbooks come with detailed video answer explanations taught by one of our fabulous instructors.

Our goal is to make your life easier, so let us know how we can help you by e-mailing us at: info@argoprep.com.

ALL RIGHTS RESERVED
Copyright © 2022 by Argo Brothers, Inc.

ISBN: 978-1951048914
Published by Argo Brothers, Inc.

All rights reserved, no part of this book may be reproduced or distributed in any form or by any means without the written permission of Argo Brothers, Inc.
All the materials within are the exclusive property of Argo Brothers, Inc.

ArgoPrep has won **over 10+ educational awards** for their workbooks and online learning platform. Here are a few highlighted awards!

TABLE OF CONTENTS

Week 1 - *Rational numbers* **11**

Week 2 - *Multiply/divide rational numbers, fractions and solve real-world word problems.* **17**

Week 3 - *Add, subtract, factor and expand algebraic expressions* . **23**

Week 4 - *Rewriting expressions.* **29**

Week 5 - *Real-world word problems* **35**

Week 6 - *Writing your own equations and inequalities* **41**

Week 7 - *Unit rates, ratios, proportions* **47**

Week 8 - *Percents (simple interest, tax, discount, markups)* **53**

Week 9 - *Statistics* **59**

Week 10 - *Comparing and understanding data sets.* **65**

Week 11 - *Measures of center and measures of variability* **71**

Week 12 - *Probability.* **77**

Week 13 - *Probability (continued)* **83**

Week 14 - *Probability: Compound events* **89**

Week 15 - *Scale models and diagrams* **95**

Week 16 - *Triangles and angles* **101**

Week 17 - *Geometry: Slicing three-dimensional figures.* **107**

Week 18 - *Area and circumference of a circle* **113**

Week 19 - *Supplementary, complementary, adjacent angles* **119**

Week 20 - *Volume and surface area* **125**

End of Year Assessment **132**

Answer Keys. **143**

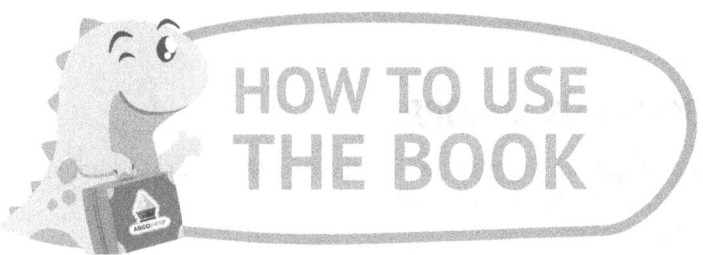

HOW TO USE THE BOOK

This workbook is designed to give lots of practice with the math Common Core State Standards (CCSS). By practicing and mastering this entire workbook, your child will become very familiar and comfortable with the state math exam. If you are a teacher using this workbook for your students, you will notice each question is labeled with the specific standard so you can easily assign your students problems in the workbook. This workbook takes the CCSS and divides them up among 20 weeks. By working on these problems on a daily basis, students will be able to (1) find any deficiencies in their understanding and/or practice of math and (2) have small successes each day that will build proficiency and confidence in their abilities.

We strongly recommend watching the videos, as they will reinforce the fundamental concepts. Please note, scrap paper may be necessary while using this workbook so that the student has sufficient space to show their work.

For a detailed overview of the Common Core State Standards for 7th grade, please visit: www.corestandards.org/Math/Content/7/introduction/

HOW TO WATCH VIDEO EXPLANATIONS
IT IS ABSOLUTELY FREE

Go to **argoprep.com/ccm7**
OR scan the QR Code:

OTHER BOOKS BY ARGOPREP

Here are some other test prep workbooks by ArgoPrep you may be interested in. All of our workbooks come equipped with detailed video explanations to make your learning experience a breeze! Visit us at *www.argoprep.com*

COMMON CORE MATH SERIES

COMMON CORE ELA SERIES

INTRODUCING MATH!

Introducing Math! by ArgoPrep is an award-winning series created by certified teachers to provide students with high-quality practice problems. Our workbooks include topic overviews with instruction, practice questions, answer explanations along with digital access to video explanations. Practice in confidence - with ArgoPrep!

SCIENCE SERIES

Science Daily Practice Workbook by ArgoPrep is an award-winning series created by certified science teachers to help build mastery of foundational science skills. Our workbooks explore science topics in depth with ArgoPrep's 5 E'S to build science mastery.

KIDS SUMMER ACADEMY SERIES

ArgoPrep's Kids Summer Academy series helps prevent summer learning loss and gets students ready for their new school year by reinforcing core foundations in math, english and science. Our workbooks also introduce new concepts so students can get a head start and be on top of their game for the new school year!

CAPTAIN BRAVERY

WATER FIRE

MYSTICAL NINJA

GREEN POISON

FIRESTORM WARRIOR

RAPID NINJA

CAPTAIN ARGO

THUNDER WARRIOR

ADRASTOS THE SUPER WARRIOR

DANCE HERO

GREEN DRAGON WARRIOR

For more practice with 7th Grade Math, be sure to check out our other book, Common Core Math Workbook Grade 7: Free Response

WEEK 1

VIDEO EXPLANATIONS

This week you will begin by using strategies to add and subtract rational numbers as well as find pairs of numbers that have a sum of zero.

You can find detailed video explanations of each problem in the book by visiting:
ArgoPrep.com/ccm7

WEEK 1 : DAY 1

1. Altitude above sea level is measured in positive values and below sea level is measured in negative values. If Andrew started at sea level and decreased his altitude by 15 meters before increasing his altitude by 8 meters, what was his final altitude?

   A. +15 meters
   B. – 7 meters
   C. – 8 meters
   D. – 15 meters

   7.NS.1

2. Below are some transactions (in dollars) that Alicia made with her bank account.

Deposits	Withdrawals
151.80	- 253.91
200	- 607.40

   If Alicia's account had $1245 before any deposits or withdrawals, what was her final balance?

   A. $383.69
   B. $735.49
   C. $1596.08
   D. $1755.23

   7.NS.1

3. Asa owed $25 to his friend. He then borrowed another $14 after paying back $12 to his sister. Which expression could be used to find how much money Asa owes or has?

   A. 25 + 14 + 12
   B. - 25 - 14 + 12
   C. - 25 + 14 - 12
   D. 25 + 14 – 12

   7.NS.1

4. Sunday morning it was −15.6°F. If the temperature dropped 3.8°F in the afternoon, what was the temperature at that point?

   A. 11.8°F
   B. 19.4°F
   C. −11.8°F
   D. -19.4°F

   7.NS.1

5. Find the value of the expression below.

   $$36.9 + 12.42 - 8.6 - 17$$

   A. 15.08
   B. 23.72
   C. 33.78
   D. 39.02

   7.NS.1

TIP of the DAY

Negative numbers can represent money a person owes, spends or withdraws.

WEEK 1 : DAY 2

1. Altitude above sea level is measured in positive values and below sea level is measured in negative values. If Ava started at 120 feet above sea level and then decreased her altitude by 214 feet, what is her altitude now?

   A. 94 feet
   B. − 334 feet
   C. − 94 feet
   D. 334 feet

   7.NS.1

2. Below are some transactions (in dollars) that Adam made with his bank account.

Deposits	Withdrawals
15.89	-325.16
113.05	-72.48

   If Adam's account had $459 before any deposits or withdrawals, what was his final balance?

   A. $61.36
   B. $190.30
   C. $197.36
   D. $727.70

   7.NS.1

3. Anna started with $61. She paid back $40 to her brother, and then her sister borrowed $5. Which expression could be used to find how much money Anna now has?

   A. 61 + 40 − 5 = 96
   B. 61 − 40 + 5 = 26
   C. − 61 − 40 − 5 = -106
   D. 61 − 40 − 5 = 16

   7.NS.1

4. Yesterday it was 61.2°F. Overnight the temperature rose 7.1°F. What was the temperature this morning?

   A. 68.3°F   C. − 68.3°F
   B. 54.1°F   D. − 54.1°F

   7.NS.1

5. Altitude above sea level is measured in positive values and below sea level is measured in negative values. If Alice started at 81 yards below sea level and then increased her altitude by 57 yards, what was her final altitude?

   A. 24 yards   C. − 138 yards
   B. − 24 yards   D. 138 yards

   7.NS.1

A person's deposits or savings are often represented by positive numbers.

WEEK 1 : DAY 3

1. Tuesday night it was 8.6°C. If the temperature rose 4°C overnight, what was the temperature Wednesday morning?

   A. 4.6°C
   B. 12.6°C
   C. − 4.6°C
   D. − 12.6°C

   7.NS.1

2. Below are the transactions (in dollars) that Alex made with his bank account last week.

   | 17.93 | -800.50 | 698.71 | -412.68 |

   If Alex's account had $1,109.52 before any deposits or withdrawals, what was his account balance at the end of the week?

   A. - $820.30
   B. $512.88
   C. $612.98
   D. $820.30

   7.NS.1

3. Altitude above sea level is measured in positive values and below sea level is measured in negative values. If Alan started at 315 feet below sea level and then decreased his altitude by 110 feet, what is his altitude now?

   A. 425 feet
   B. 205 feet
   C. − 205 feet
   D. − 425 feet

   7.NS.1

4. At the beginning of the month Asher had $1609 for his expenses. If his rent was $647, groceries were $213 and utilities were $194, how much money would have available for spending or saving at the end of the month?

   A. $455
   B. $485
   C. $555
   D. $585

   7.NS.1

5. In Petosky, Michigan it was −12.8°F. In Bay City Michigan the temperature was 7.9°F. How much colder was it in Petosky?

   A. − 4.9°F colder
   B. 4.9°F colder
   C. 5.1°F colder
   D. 20.7°F colder

   7.NS.1

6. Thursday night it was −5.1°C. If the temperature dropped 1.9°C overnight, what was the temperature Friday morning?

   A. − 7°C
   B. −3.2°C
   C. 3.2°C
   D. 7°C

   7.NS.1

TIP of the DAY

When adding numbers that have different signs, take the difference between the numbers themselves (or magnitude) and keep the sign of the number with the larger magnitude.

WEEK 1 : DAY 4

1. What is the decimal equivalent of $\frac{1}{8}$?

   A. 0.125
   B. 0.18
   C. 1.8
   D. 8.1

   7.NS.2

2. What is the product of $\left(\frac{-3}{8}\right) \times \left(-\frac{2}{5}\right)$?

   A. $\frac{-3}{20}$
   B. $\frac{3}{20}$
   C. $\frac{-6}{13}$
   D. $\frac{-4}{40}$

   7.NS.2

3. Convert $\frac{5}{6}$ to its decimal equivalent using long division.

   A. $0.8\overline{3}$
   B. $0.\overline{83}$
   C. 5.6
   D. 6.5

   7.NS.2

4. What is the decimal equivalent $\frac{7}{9}$?

   A. 0.97
   B. 0.79
   C. $0.\overline{7}$
   D. 0.7

   7.NS.2

5. What is the product of $\left(\frac{5}{7}\right) \times \left(-\frac{3}{7}\right)$?

   A. $\frac{3}{5}$
   B. $\frac{-5}{3}$
   C. $\frac{15}{49}$
   D. $-\frac{15}{49}$

   7.NS.2

6. Arnold is subtracting 12 from 19. Which equation could be used to find the difference between 19 and 12?

   A. 12 − 19
   B. 12 + (− 19)
   C. 19 + (− 12)
   D. − 19 + (− 12)

   7.NS.1

TIP of the DAY

If 2 (or more) numbers have the same sign, you can add those numbers and keep that sign so
− 8 + (− 17) = − 25.

WEEK 1 : DAY 5

ASSESSMENT

1. Below are some transactions that Anastasia made to her bank account.

Deposits	Withdrawals
309.65	400
81.27	512.30

   If Anastasia's account had $478.36 before any deposits or withdrawals, what was her final balance?

   A. - $43.02
   B. $78.32
   C. $390.92
   D. $912.30

   7.NS.1

2. Altitude above sea level is measured in positive values and below sea level is measured in negative values. If Arial started at 907 feet below sea level and then increased her altitude by 452 feet, what is her altitude now?

   A. – 455 feet
   B. – 1,359 feet
   C. 455 feet
   D. 1,359 feet

   7.NS.1

3. Bella is subtracting 17 from 11. Which equation could be used to find the difference between 11 and 17?

   A. 11 + 17
   B. 11 + (– 17)
   C. 17 + (– 11)
   D. – 17 + (– 11)

   7.NS.1

4. Convert $\frac{9}{11}$ to its decimal equivalent.

   A. 0.81
   B. $0.8\overline{1}$
   C. $0.\overline{81}$
   D. $0.\overline{91}$

   7.NS.2

5. What is the decimal equivalent of $\frac{4}{5}$?

   A. 0.4
   B. 0.45
   C. 0.5
   D. 0.8

   7.NS.2

DAY 6
Challenge question

Saturday night it was −17°C. If the temperature rose 12.5°C overnight, what was the temperature Sunday morning?

7.NS.1

16

WEEK 2

VIDEO EXPLANATIONS

Week 2 will allow you to practice multiplying and dividing rational numbers, including fractions. You can also use different properties of operations to solve real-world problems that involve all 4 operations. You will also be able to check your conversions as you change fractions to decimals.

You can find detailed video explanations of each problem in the book by visiting:
ArgoPrep.com/ccm7

WEEK 2 : DAY 1

1. Convert $\frac{507}{1000}$ to its decimal equivalent.

   A. 0.57
   B. 0.507
   C. 5.07
   D. 50.7

   7.NS.2

2. What is the decimal equivalent of $\frac{12}{15}$?

   A. 0.03
   B. 0.1215
   C. 0.8
   D. 12.15

   7.NS.2

3. What is the product of $\left(-\frac{12}{14}\right) \times \left(-\frac{11}{15}\right)$?

   A. $-\frac{22}{35}$
   B. $\frac{22}{35}$
   C. $-\frac{121}{210}$
   D. $\frac{121}{210}$

   7.NS.2

4. Below are the transactions that Arik made with his bank account last week.

   | -148.03 | -90.25 | -68.43 | 921.87 |

   If Arik's account had $651.20 before any deposits or withdrawals, what was his account balance at the end of the week?

   A. $306.71
   B. $615.16
   C. $966.31
   D. $1266.36

   7.NS.1

5. What is the decimal equivalent of $\frac{3}{8}$?

   A. 0.375
   B. 0.38
   C. $0.\overline{38}$
   D. $0.3\overline{8}$

   7.NS.2

6. What is the product of $\left(\frac{-2}{5}\right) \times \left(\frac{8}{3}\right)$?

   A. $\frac{-3}{20}$
   B. $\frac{-6}{40}$
   C. $\frac{-15}{16}$
   D. $\frac{-16}{15}$

   7.NS.2

TIP of the DAY

Many fractions that are changed to decimals will either terminate or repeat.

WEEK 2 : DAY 2

1. What is the decimal equivalent of $\frac{14}{5}$?

   A. 0.35
   B. 1.45
   C. 2.8
   D. 14.5

   7.NS.2

2. What is the product of $\left(-\frac{10}{3}\right) \times \left(-\frac{1}{7}\right)$?

   A. $\frac{10}{21}$
   B. $-\frac{10}{21}$
   C. $\frac{11}{10}$
   D. $\frac{-11}{10}$

   7.NS.2

3. Find the value of the expression below.

   $$-171 + 61.29 + 91.4 - 84.7$$

   A. − 103.01
   B. − 238.99
   C. 103.01
   D. 238.99

   7.NS.1

4. There are 25 students in Mrs. Boyer's homeroom. Twelve of those students are boys. Write the fraction of boys as a decimal number.

   A. 0.25
   B. 0.48
   C. 0.5
   D. $2.08\overline{3}$

   7.NS.2

5. Which number is NOT equal to $\frac{3}{5}$?

   A. $\frac{6}{10}$
   B. 0.60
   C. 0.06
   D. 0.6

   7.NS.1

6. Altitude above sea level is measured in positive values and below sea level is measured in negative values. If Anthony started at − 8 yards altitude and then decreased his altitude by 13 yards, what was his final altitude?

   A. +5 yards
   B. + 21 yards
   C. − 5 yards
   D. − 21 yards

   7.NS.1

To find the decimal equivalent of a fraction, divide the numerator by the denominator.

WEEK 2 : DAY 3

1. Three boys bought some apples to share. Each pound of apples was $2.69. They bought 9 pounds of apples. If they also shared the price, how much money would each boy contribute?

   A. $6.05
   B. $8.07
   C. $12.11
   D. $24.21

   7.NS.3

2. Bonita makes $11.75/hour and Bruce makes $12.50/hour. If Bonita worked 25 hours and Bruce worked 19 hours, what was the difference in the amount of money they each earned?

   A. $293.75
   B. $237.50
   C. $56.25
   D. $18.75

   7.NS.3

3. Barbie went to the store and bought 11 packages of chicken and 15 packages of beef. If the beef cost $4.59 per package and the chicken was $1.98 per package, what was the cost for all of the meat?

   A. $80.19
   B. $90.63
   C. $89.37
   D. $100.37

   7.NS.3

4. Five days last month it rained 6.5 inches. It rained 3.5 inches on 7 days last month. How many inches did it rain on those 12 days?

   A. 24 inches
   B. 32.5 inches
   C. 46.5 inches
   D. 57 inches

   7.NS.3

5. Monday night it was −2.3°C. If the temperature dropped 2.3°C overnight, what was the temperature Tuesday morning?

   A. −4.6°C
   B. 0°C
   C. 4.6°C
   D. 6.4°C

   7.NS.1

6. Benjamin ran 8.7 miles each weekday last week and 12.9 miles each day of the weekend. What was the total distance Benjamin ran last week?

   A. 60.9 miles
   B. 69.3 miles
   C. 77.6 miles
   D. 86.7 miles

   7.NS.3

TIP of the DAY

In word problems, try to find the correct operation(s) to use. It may help to use smaller numbers to check the operation first and then use the numbers given in the problem.

WEEK 2 : DAY 4

1. Bryce did chores every single day in September. It took Bryce $\frac{7}{8}$ hours to complete his chores on 20 of the days. The remaining days of the month it took him 1 hour to complete his chores. How many hours did Bryce do chores in September? (There are 30 days in September).

   A. 26.25 hours C. 28.5 hours
   B. 27.5 hours   D. 28.75 hours

   7.NS.3

2. Brenda talked on the phone for 3.1 hours on Monday, Friday and Sunday. The other days of the week she only talked 1.85 hours. How much time did Brenda talk on the phone last week?

   A. 16.7 hours   C. 22.25 hours
   B. 19.8 hours   D. 34.65 hours

   7.NS.3

3. On his trip, Buddy drove 60 mph for 1 hour, 55 mph for 3 hours and 40 mph for 2 hours. What was the distance of Buddy's trip?

   A. 155 miles   C. 250 miles
   B. 210 miles   D. 305 miles

   7.NS.3

4. Althea owed $451.26 on her credit card. She made a payment of $395 and then charged another $506.13. What does Althea still owe on her credit card?

   A. $340.13   C. $902.52
   B. $562.39   D. $1,352.39

   7.NS.3

5. Addison began her hike at 1,986 feet above sea level. She then hiked down 2,510 feet, decreased her altitude by another 420 feet and then increased her altitude by 712 feet. What is Addison's final altitude?

   A. – 4,204 feet C. 608 feet
   B. – 232 feet   D. 5,628 feet

   7.NS.1

6. Brent was writing a paper. He typed 942 words and then had to delete a paragraph that contained 310 words. He wrote another 2 pages that each contained 524 words. How many words are in Brent's paper now?

   A. 1,680 words   C. 1,990 words
   B. 1,776 words   D. 2,300 words

   7.NS.3

TIP of the DAY

It is always a good idea to check your answers to make sure they are reasonable.

WEEK 2 : DAY 5

ASSESSMENT

1. For her wedding, Brooke had 275 cupcakes that cost $1.50 each. She served 234 people dinners that were $19.78 each. The DJ and photographer cost $750 each and the hall was $4,213. What was the total cost for Brooke's wedding reception?

   A. $10,004.02 C. $10,754.02
   B. $10,692.52 D. $11,565.00

   7.NS.3

2. Baby Alene slept for $\frac{4}{5}$ of an hour in the morning, slept for 1.7 hours at naptime and fell asleep again in the afternoon for another 90 minutes. How much time was Baby Alene asleep?

   A. 3.8 hours   C. 228 minutes
   B. 4 hours   D. 400 minutes

   7.NS.3

3. A hummingbird flies forward 219 meters, backwards 45 meters and forward 25 meters. Which equation can be used to find how far forward the hummingbird flew?

   A. 219 + 25 − 45 = 199
   B. 219 + 45 − 25 = 239
   C. 219 − 25 − 45 = 149
   D. 219 + 25 + 45 = 289

   7.NS.1

4. At Lake Ann Camp it costs $449 for a Junior camper, $489 for a Fresh Start camper and $510 for a Reborne Ranger. If there are 25 Junior campers, 9 Fresh Start campers and 3 Reborne Rangers, what is the total cost for these camp registrations?

   A. $16,707
   B. $17,156
   C. $17,645
   D. $18,093

   7.NS.3

5. In Lakeland, Florida it was 72.8°F but the temperature dropped 17.9°F. Now what is the temperature in Lakeland?

   A. −54.9°F
   B. −90.7°F
   C. 54.9°F
   D. 90.7°Ft

   7.NS.1

6. What is the product of $\left(-\frac{9}{10}\right) \times \left(-\frac{3}{5}\right)$?

   A. $\frac{3}{2}$ C. $\frac{27}{50}$

   B. $\frac{-3}{2}$ D. $\frac{-27}{50}$

   7.NS.2

DAY 6
Challenge question

At the beginning of the month Augustus had $3,596 for his expenses. He budgeted $1,075 for his mortgage, $392 for groceries, $279 for utilities and $194 for entertainment. If he stuck to his budget, how much money would he have available at the end of the month?

7.NS.1

WEEK 3

This week you will be able to add, subtract, factor and expand algebraic expressions using the properties of operations.

You can find detailed video explanations of each problem in the book by visiting:
ArgoPrep.com/ccm7

WEEK 3 : DAY 1

1. Which expression represents a factorization of 16a − 24ab?

   A. 8a (2 - 3b)
   B. 2a (4 - 3b)
   C. 8 (2a - 3b)
   D. 8a (2a - 3b)

   7.EE.1

2. Which property is shown below?

   (7s + 10t) + 3t = 7s + (10t + 3t)

   A. Associative Property
   B. Commutative Property
   C. Distributive Property
   D. Inverse Property

   7.EE.1

3. Which expression is equivalent to: (7d + 3) - (8 - 5d)?

   A. 2d - 5
   B. 2d + 5
   C. 12d - 11
   D. 12d - 5

   7.EE.1

4. Which expression represents a factorization of 125f + 75fg?

   A. 25f + 3
   B. 5 + 3g
   C. 25f (5 + 3g)
   D. 25fg (5 + 3g)

   7.EE.1

5. What is the value of the expression below?

   360.91 − 242.5 − 98.03 − 127

   A. − 106.62
   B. − 237.36
   C. − 467.53
   D. − 828.44

   7.NS.1

6. Which expression is equivalent to: (h - 5) + (6h - 4)?

   A. 7h - 9
   B. 7h^2 - 9
   C. 7h + 9
   D. 5h - 7

   7.EE.1

TIP of the DAY: After factoring, you can check your answer by multiplying the factors to see if you get an expression that is the same as the original expression.

WEEK 3 : DAY 2

1. Which property is shown below?

   $5u \times (8v \times 7w) = (8v \times 7w) 5u$

   A. Associative Property
   B. Commutative Property
   C. Distributive Property
   D. Inverse Property

   7.EE.1

2. Which expression represents a factorization of $27km - 24k$?

   A. $2k(7m - 12)$
   B. $3k(9m - 8)$
   C. $3k(9m - 6)$
   D. $9k(3m - 2)$

   7.EE.1

3. Which expression is NOT equivalent to $4 - 10e + 7e - 13$?

   A. $-3e - 9$
   B. $-3(e + 3)$
   C. $-1(3e + 9)$
   D. $-1(3e - 9)$

   7.EE.1

Use the steps below to answer questions 4 – 5.

Step 1: $\frac{2}{3}(15a + 27b + 9a - 12a)$

Step 2: $10a + 18b + 6a - 8a$

Step 3: $10a + 18b + (6a - 8a)$

Step 4: $8a + 18b$

4. Which property below is used between Steps 1 and 2?

   A. Associative Property
   B. Commutative Property
   C. Distributive Property
   D. Identity Property

   7.EE.1

5. Which property below is used between Steps 2 and 3?

   A. Associative Property
   B. Commutative Property
   C. Identity Property
   D. Inverse Property

   7.EE.1

TIP of the DAY

An example of the Distributive Property is $7(z - 10) = 7z - 70$.

WEEK 3 : DAY 3

Use the steps below to answer questions 1 – 2.

Step 1: $\frac{3}{4}(12x + 20y)$

Step 2: $9x + 15y$

Step 3: $3(3x + 5y)$

Step 4: $3(5y + 3x)$

3. Which expression is equivalent to:

$$c - 15c - 10 + 12c - 8?$$

   A. $2c + 18$
   B. $2c - 18$
   C. $-2c - 18$
   D. $-2c + 18$

   7.EE.1

1. Which property below is used between Steps 1 and 2?

   A. Associative Property
   B. Commutative Property
   C. Distributive Property
   D. Identity Property

   7.EE.1

4. Which expression represents a factorization of $105np + 80npq$?

   A. $5np(21p + 16q)$
   B. $15np(7 + 5)$
   C. $5np(21 + 16q)$
   D. $15n(21p + 6q)$

   7.EE.1

2. Which property below is used between Steps 3 and 4?

   A. Associative Property
   B. Commutative Property
   C. Identity Property
   D. Inverse Property

   7.EE.1

5. Yesterday it was −4.2°C. Overnight the temperature dropped 5.9°C. What was the temperature this morning?

   A. 1.4°C
   B. 1.7°C
   C. −1.7°C
   D. −10.1°C

   7.NS.1

TIP of the DAY

When there is a negative sign to the left of a set of parentheses, every term within the parentheses is subtracted.

WEEK 3 : DAY 4

1. Which expression represents a factorization of $56xyz - 16xy + 24xz$?

    A. $8x(7xyz - 2y + 3z)$
    B. $16x(4yz - y + 2z)$
    C. $4x(19yz - 4y + 8z)$
    D. $8x(7yz - 2y + 3z)$

    7.EE.1

2. Which property is shown in the expression below?

    $$7ab(5 - 8c) = 35ab - 56abc$$

    A. Associative Property
    B. Commutative Property
    C. Distributive Property
    D. Identity Property

    7.EE.1

3. What is the product of $\left(\frac{21}{14}\right) \times \left(-\frac{11}{12}\right)$?

    A. $-\frac{11}{18}$
    B. $-1\frac{3}{8}$
    C. $-1\frac{3}{7}$
    D. $-1\frac{7}{11}$

    7.NS.2

4. Which expression is equivalent to $1.3m - 14.5n + 11.8m + 8.6n$?

    A. $13.1m - 5.9n$
    B. $13.1m + 5.9n$
    C. $10.5m - 5.9n$
    D. $10.5m + 5.9n$

    7.EE.1

5. Which expression represents a factorization of $3q - 5qr + 4pq$?

    A. $\frac{1}{3}q(1 - 15r + 12p)$
    B. $\frac{1}{2}(1.5q - 2.5r + 2p)$
    C. $\frac{1}{4}q(12 - 20r + 16p)$
    D. $\frac{1}{6}q(2q - 0.8r + 24p)$

    7.EE.1

6. What is the decimal equivalent of $\frac{3}{12}$?

    A. 0.4
    B. 0.5
    C. 0.25
    D. 0.312

    7.NS.2

TIP of the DAY

An example of the Commutative Property is:
$4x + 5y + z = z + 4x + 5y$.

WEEK 3 : DAY 5

ASSESSMENT

1. Which expression is equivalent to:

   $8.5p + 3.6q - (9.8q - 2.1p)$?

   A. $10.6p - 6.2q$
   B. $6.4p - 6.2q$
   C. $1.3p - 1.5q$
   D. $1.3p + 5.7q$

   7.EE.1

2. Which expression is NOT equivalent to the other three expressions?

   A. $\frac{2}{5}t(40s + 15 - 5u)$
   B. $2t(8s + 3 - u)$
   C. $\frac{1}{5}t(20s + 30 - u)$
   D. $16st + 6t - 2tu$

   7.EE.1

Use the steps below to answer questions 3 – 4.

Step 1: $30ab + 45ac - 25ad + 20ab$

Step 2: $30ab + 20ab + 45ac - 25ad$

Step 3: $50ab + 45ac - 25ad$

Step 4: $5a(10b + 9c - 5d)$

3. Which property below is used between Steps 1 and 2?

   A. Associative Property
   B. Commutative Property
   C. Distributive Property
   D. Identity Property

   7.EE.1

4. Which property below is used between Steps 3 and 4?

   A. Associative Property
   B. Commutative Property
   C. Distributive Property
   D. Identity Property

   7.EE.1

5. Which expression is equivalent to $\frac{4}{5}(v - 5w + 7)$?

   A. $\frac{4}{5}v - 20w + \frac{28}{5}$
   B. $4v - w + 28$
   C. $\frac{4}{5v} - \frac{4}{25}w + \frac{28}{5}$
   D. $\frac{4}{5}v - 4w + \frac{28}{5}$

   7.EE.1

DAY 6
Challenge question

What is the factorization of $36a - 18ab + 27ac$?

7.EE.1

28

Now that you know how to factor and expand expressions, in Week 4 you will be able to rewrite expressions in different forms so you can better understand a problem as well as its context.

**You can find detailed video explanations of each problem in the book by visiting:
ArgoPrep.com/ccm7**

WEEK 4 : DAY 1

1. The cost of camp, c, is going to increase by 6% next summer. Which expression represents the expected cost for next summer's camp?

   A. $c + 0.6$
   B. $0.06c$
   C. $1 + 0.06c$
   D. $c + 0.06c$

   7.EE.2

3. Which statement is true about the rectangle's length?

   A. The length is 3 times the width.
   B. The length is 3 inches more than the width.
   C. The length is 4 times the width.
   D. The length is 4 inches more than the width.

   7.EE.2

Use the diagram below to answer questions 2 – 3. The rectangle shown is measured in inches where m is the width.

4. Bree bought a dress that was discounted 23%. If the non-sale price was d, which expression represents the cost Bree paid for the dress?

   A. $d - 0.23$ C. $1 - 0.23$
   B. $1 - 0.23d$ D. $d - 0.23d$

   7.EE.2

5. What is the decimal equivalent of $\frac{5}{4}$?

   A. 0.45   C. 1.2
   B. 0.8   D. 1.25

   7.NS.2

2. Which statement is true about the rectangle's perimeter?

   A. The perimeter is 3 times the width.
   B. The perimeter is 3 inches more than the width.
   C. The perimeter is 8 times the width.
   D. The perimeter is 8 inches more than the width.

   7.EE.2

6. The number of employees is expected to increase by 11.5% next quarter. If e represents the current number of employees, which expression represents the expected number of employees?

   A. $e + 11.5e$ C. $1 + 0.115e$
   B. $1.115e$ D. $e + 0.115$

   7.EE.2

TIP of the DAY

When working with percentages, remember that the original amount is 100% and all increases and decreases are based upon that original amount.

30

WEEK 4 : DAY 2

1. A shirt originally was priced at s. Chester bought it at a 7% discount. Which expression represents the cost Chester paid for the shirt?

   A. 0.07s + s
   B. 0.93s
   C. s − 0.07
   D. 1 − 0.07s

3. Which statement is true about the rectangle's perimeter?

   A. The perimeter is 2.5 times the length.
   B. The perimeter is 2.5 meters more than the length.
   C. The perimeter is 8 times the width.
   D. The perimeter is 8 meters more than the width.

Use the diagram below to answer questions 2 – 3. The rectangle shown is measured in meters and the width is represented by w.

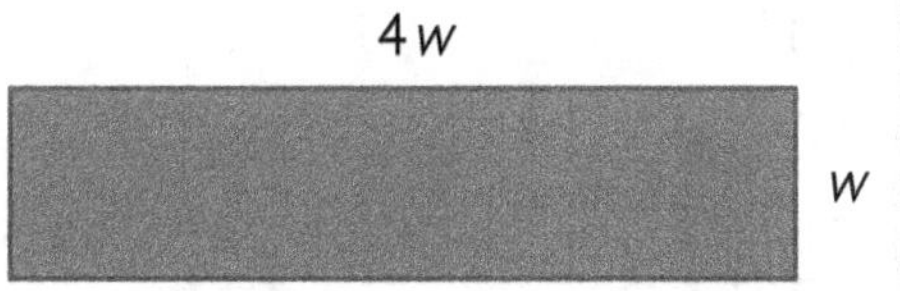

4w

w

4. Which expression is equivalent to
   $(10x - 3y) - (8y - x)$?

   A. 2x − 4y
   B. 9x − 11y
   C. 2x − 2y
   D. 11x − 11y

2. Which statement is true about the rectangle's length?

   A. The length is 3 times the width.
   B. The length is 3 inches more than the width.
   C. The length is 4 times the width.
   D. The length is 4 inches more than the width.

5. The store bought golf clubs that cost g dollars. The store marked up the clubs so they were 33% higher than what they bought them for. Which expression shows the new cost of the golf clubs?

   A. 1 + 0.33g   C. g + 0.33
   B. 0.33g   D. g + 0.33g

TIP of the DAY

A discount or decrease will mean less than 100% of the original number.

31

WEEK 4 : DAY 3

1. The original cost of the tire was *t* and it was not on sale. However, there was an $8\frac{1}{2}$% sales tax. What is the cost of the tire including tax?

   A. $t + 0.85t$
   B. $1 + 0.85t$
   C. $t + 0.085t$
   D. $t + 0.085$

   7.EE.2

3. Which statement is true about the rectangle's perimeter?

   A. The perimeter is 10 times the width.
   B. The perimeter is 10 yards more than the width.
   C. The perimeter is 4 times the height.
   D. The perimeter is 4 yards more than the height.

   7.EE.2

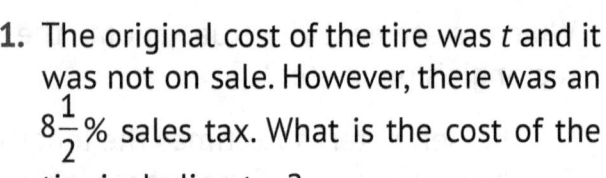

Use the diagram to answer questions 2 – 3.

The rectangle shown is measured in yards and the height is represented by *h*. The other dimension is the width.

4. The original price of the shoes was *s*. If Bogdan had a coupon for 15% off, what was the sale price of the shoes?

   A. $0.15s$
   B. $s - 0.15$
   C. $1 - 0.15s$
   D. $s - 0.15s$

   7.EE.2

2. Which statement is true about the rectangle's height?

   A. The height is 4 yards more than the width.
   B. The height is 4 times the width.
   C. The height is 5 times the width.
   D. The height is 5 yards more than the width.

   7.EE.2

5. Beck makes $12.13 an hour and Charles makes $9.50 an hour. If Beck worked 21 hours and Charles worked 32 hours, how much money did they earn altogether?

   A. $254.73
   B. $304.00
   C. $558.73
   D. $692.16

   7.NS.2

TIP of the DAY

An increase or markup means more than 100% of the original number.

32

WEEK 4 : DAY 4

1. The music store bought a violin that cost v dollars. The store marked up the violin so it was 54% higher than what they bought it for. Which expression shows the new cost of the violin?

   A. $v + 0.54v$
   B. $1 + 0.54v$
   C. $v + 0.54$
   D. $0.54v$

   7.EE.2

2. The population of Moore Haven, M, is expected to decrease by 3% over the next 10 years. Which expression shows the expected population of Moore Haven in 10 years?

   A. $M - 0.03$
   B. 0.97
   C. $M - 0.03M$
   D. $1 - 0.03M$

   7.EE.2

3. Which statement is true about the rectangle's length?

   A. The length is 4 centimeters longer than the width.
   B. The length is 4 times longer the width.
   C. The length is 5 times longer the width.
   D. The length is 5 centimeters longer than the width.

   7.EE.2

4. Which statement is true about the rectangle's perimeter?

   A. The perimeter is 6 times the width.
   B. The perimeter is 6 centimeters more than the width.
   C. The perimeter is 12 times the width.
   D. The perimeter is 12 centimeters more than the width.

   7.EE.2

Use the diagram below to answer questions 3 – 4. The rectangle shown is measured in centimeters and the width is represented by a. The other dimension is the length.

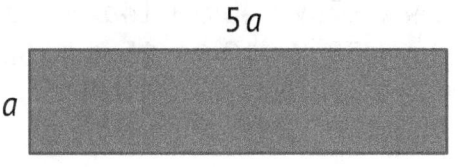

5. Caroline has a discount card that gives her 4% off the purchase of each pizza. If p is the cost of a regular pizza, how much does Caroline pay for her pizza?

   A. $p - 0.4$
   B. $0.96p$
   C. $p - 0.04$
   D. $1 - 0.04p$

   7.EE.2

TIP of the DAY

Percent problems assume that the original number is valued at 100%.

WEEK 4 : DAY 5

ASSESSMENT

1. The current tuition, t, at State College is expected to rise $12\frac{1}{2}$ % over the next few years. What will the tuition be after that increase?

   A. t + 0.125
   B. 1 + 0.125t
   C. 1.125
   D. t + 0.125t

   7.EE.2

Use the diagram to answer questions 2 – 3.
The rectangle shown is measured in inches where h is the height (or length). The other dimension is the width

7.EE.2

2. Which statement is true about the rectangle's perimeter?

   A. The perimeter is 3 times the height.
   B. The perimeter is 3 inches more than the height.
   C. The perimeter is 6 times the height.
   D. The perimeter is 6 inches more than the height.

   x.xx.x

3. Which statement is true about the rectangle's height?

   A. The height is $\frac{1}{2}$ the width.
   B. The height is $\frac{1}{2}$ an inch more than the width.
   C. The height is 2 times the width.
   D. The height is 2 inches more than the width.

   7.EE.2

4. If the number of honeybees, b, is expected to decrease by $6\frac{2}{5}$ %, which expression represents the number of honey bees after the decrease?

   A. b – 0.64
   B. b – 0.064b
   C. b – 0.064
   D. 1 – 0.064b

   7.EE.2

5. Which expression is NOT equivalent to: $28ax - 7ay + 35az$?

   A. 14ax – 7ay + 40az + 14ax – 5az
   B. 8ay + 28ax + 10az – 15ay + 25az
   C. –7a (-4x + y - 5z)
   D. 7a (4x + y + 5z)

   7.EE.1

DAY 6
Challenge question

Betsie bought a purse that was discounted 15%. Use p to equal the regular price of the purse and write an expression that shows how much Betise paid for her purse.

7.EE.2

WEEK 5

Week 5 lets you find answers to real-world problems that require many steps. You will use positive and negative rational numbers to solve these problems and also to check your answers to see if they make sense.

You can find detailed video explanations of each problem in the book by visiting:
ArgoPrep.com/ccm7

WEEK 5 : DAY 1

1. A pair of shoes that regularly sell for $105 are on sale for 45% off the regular price. What is the sale price?

   A. $47.25
   B. $57.75
   C. $60.00
   D. $62.50

   7.EE.3

2. Messy Essy very rarely cleaned off her table. She started with $3\frac{5}{8}$ inches of mail piled up, and she added $\frac{3}{4}$ inches of mail each day. How tall will the pile of mail be after 5 days?

   A. $6\frac{5}{8}$ inches
   B. $7\frac{3}{8}$ inches
   C. $8\frac{3}{4}$ inches
   D. $8\frac{19}{20}$ inches

   7.EE.3

3. Elisha recorded the temperature for 5 days. When he added the 5 temperatures together he got a sum of −7.4°C. If he recorded these numbers: −8.1°C, −7.4°C, 5.5°C, 6.2°C but was missing 1 record, what was the missing temperature?

   A. −8.1°C
   B. −3.6°C
   C. −1.9°C
   D. 2.3°C

   7.EE.3

4. Dierks made $13.50 per hour. He got a new job in which he made 8% more. How much did he make per hour at his new job?

   A. $14.58
   B. $17.35
   C. $21.50
   D. $24.30

   7.EE.3

5. Which expression is NOT equivalent to $-15f - f + 10g - 2g + 8f$?

   A. $-8(f + g)$
   B. $8g - 8f$
   C. $-8f + 8g$
   D. $8(g - f)$

   7.EE.1

6. The massaging chair at the airport cost $5.25 for every 10 minutes. The chair was used for $\frac{1}{2}$ an hour in the morning, 20 minutes in the afternoon and 3 hours and 40 minutes in the evening. How much money should have been deposited into the chair that day?

   A. $23.63
   B. $136.50
   C. $141.75
   D. $147.00

   7.EE.3

TIP of the DAY

To add or subtract decimal numbers, remember to line up the decimal points vertically first.

WEEK 5 : DAY 2

1. Ellie earns $11.35 per hour. Below you can see how many hours she worked last week. How much did Ellie earn last week? Round your answer to the nearest cent.

Wednesday	$4\frac{1}{8}$
Friday	$8\frac{1}{2}$
Saturday	$7\frac{7}{8}$
Sunday	$5\frac{3}{4}$

A. $287.98
B. $289.43
C. $297.48
D. $297.94

7.EE.3

2. Chicken is normally $2.15/lb. but if you purchase 26 pounds for $41.34, how much do you save per pound?

A. $0.19
B. $0.26
C. $0.56
D. $0.79

7.EE.3

3. Each day Davey went golfing. His scores were – 8, 4, 3, 0 and – 1. What was his average score?

A. 0
B. $-\frac{2}{5}$
C. $-\frac{1}{2}$
D. $-\frac{7}{9}$

7.EE.3

4. Esme's tire had a leak. It originally held 30 pounds of pressure but was losing 1.8 pounds of pressure each hour. How many pounds of pressure would there be after 7 hours?

A. 12.6
B. 17.4
C. 21
D. 28.2

7.EE.3

5. Which property below is shown in the equation below?

$(3a + 5a) + 12a = 3a + (5a + 12a)$

A. Associative Property
B. Commutative Property
C. Distributive Property
D. Inverse Property

7.EE.1

TIP of the DAY

There are terminating and repeating decimals that are not equal. $\frac{1}{3}$ = 0.333... which is NOT the same as 0.3.

WEEK 5 : DAY 3

1. Dixon kept record of the temperature for 5 days. He recorded these numbers: −1.1°C, 3.5°C, −4.4°C, −0.5°C, 2.7°C. What was the average of the temperatures Dixon recorded?

   A. −0.2°C
   B. −0.04°C
   C. 0.04°C
   D. 0.2°C

   7.EE.3

2. Drake made $21.75 per hour until he was laid off. Then he took another job for 12% less. What is his new hourly rate?

   A. $17.26
   B. $19.14
   C. $22.01
   D. $24.36

   7.EE.3

3. Elaine earns $9.50 for the first $10\frac{1}{2}$ hours she works and $10.30 for every hour after that. If Elaine worked $20\frac{1}{4}$ hours, how much would she earn?

   A. $192.38
   B. $200.18
   C. $208.58
   D. $210.48

   7.EE.3

4. Ezra planted 10 plants and the depth of each plant (in inches) is shown below.

   $3\frac{1}{2}$ $4\frac{1}{4}$ $2\frac{7}{8}$ $3\frac{1}{2}$ $2\frac{1}{4}$ $1\frac{7}{8}$ $2\frac{7}{8}$ $2\frac{1}{4}$ $4\frac{1}{4}$ $3\frac{3}{8}$

   What is the average depth of the plants?

   A. 3 inches
   B. $3\frac{1}{4}$ inches
   C. $3\frac{1}{8}$ inches
   D. $3\frac{1}{10}$ inches

   7.EE.3

5. Daria kept track of the temperature for several weeks. Her results are shown below. If her temperatures had a sum of −11.2°F, what is the missing temperature?

Number of days	Temperature
12	−1.3°F
5	4.8°F
8	−2°F
3	−3.5°F
1	?

   A. −4.5°F
   B. 6.9°F
   C. 13.2°F
   D. 77.3°F

   7.NS.3

TIP of the DAY

Recall the different rules for adding signed numbers and multiplying signed numbers. Be careful of the signs − they have meaning.

WEEK 5 : DAY 4

1. The fish tank could hold 25 gallons of water. It was leaking $\frac{1}{2}$ a gallon every hour. How long before the tank would be empty?

   A. 12.5 hours
   B. 25 hours
   C. 50 hours
   D. 125 hours

   7.EE.3

2. Eden and Eva's mom kept track of how much each sister grew every 4 months. Eden grew $1\frac{1}{2}$, $\frac{7}{8}$ and 2 inches and Eva grew $1\frac{3}{4}$, $1\frac{1}{4}$, and $1\frac{1}{8}$ inches. How much more did one sister grow than the other?

   A. $\frac{1}{2}$ of an inch
   B. $\frac{1}{4}$ of an inch
   C. $\frac{1}{8}$ of an inch
   D. $\frac{1}{10}$ of an inch

   7.EE.3

3. Eliza needs some material for some dresses she is making. The chart below shows how many dresses she is making and how many yards of material she needs for one dress. How much material does Eliza need in total?

Pattern	Number of Dresses	Material needed / Dresses
A	5	$5\frac{1}{4}$ yards
B	6	$4\frac{2}{3}$ yards
C	3	$6\frac{1}{3}$ yards

   A. $54\frac{1}{4}$
   B. $73\frac{1}{4}$
   C. $73\frac{11}{12}$
   D. $74\frac{1}{4}$

   7.EE.3

4. Fiona was playing a game. She started on space #8. The cards told her to move forward 12 spaces, back 10 spaces, back 1 space and then forward 5. Now which space is Fiona on?

   A. Space 11
   B. Space 14
   C. Space 23
   D. Space 36

   7.EE.3

TIP of the DAY

Negative numbers may represent loss, decrease or a measurement below a certain level.

39

WEEK 5 : DAY 5

ASSESSMENT

1. A jacket normally sells for $127. It was on sale for 18% off the regular price. What was the sale price?

   A. $104.14
   B. $109.00
   C. $111.76
   D. $149.86

   7.EE.3

2. Each football ticket is $13.50. If you purchase the season pass, you can go to 10 games for $99. How much would you save per ticket by purchasing the season pass?

   A. $3.60
   B. $4.65
   C. $6.50
   D. $8.55

   7.EE.3

3. A weight loss contestant weighed 142.3 kg. The amount of weight he gained or lost is shown below. What was his final weight?

Lost	$10\frac{1}{3}$ kg
Lost	$9\frac{3}{4}$ kg
Gained	$2\frac{1}{3}$ kg
Lost	$5\frac{1}{2}$ kg

   A. 114.38 kg
   B. 116.67 kg
   C. 117.93 kg
   D. 119.05 kg

   7.EE.3

4. Francesca earns $18.74 per hour. Below you can see how many hours she worked last week. How much did Francesca earn last week? Round to the nearest cent.

Monday	$7\frac{1}{3}$ hr
Tuesday	$5\frac{1}{2}$ hr
Thursday	$9\frac{7}{8}$ hr
Friday	$10\frac{2}{3}$ hr

   A. $580.94
   B. $598.04
   C. $618.05
   D. $625.45

   7.EE.3

5. What is the decimal equivalent of $\frac{5}{6}$?

   A. 0.8
   B. 0.83
   C. $0.8\overline{3}$
   D. $0.\overline{83}$

   7.NS.2

DAY 6
Challenge question

Franklin can dig $3\frac{3}{8}$ feet each day to get to the bottom of the well. If he starts digging at $2\frac{1}{3}$ feet down and digs for 5 days, how far down will he have dug?

7.EE.3

WEEK 6

By now you're familiar with solving real-world problems. This week you will be able to write your own equations and/or inequalities to solve these problems. You will also begin to solve linear equations by determining what steps to take first.

You can find detailed video explanations of each problem in the book by visiting:
ArgoPrep.com/ccm7

WEEK 6 : DAY 1

1. The bus charged $4.50 for a ride plus $1.25 per mile. How many complete miles could Frank travel for $20?

   A. 12
   B. 13
   C. 15
   D. 16

   7.EE.4

2. Which equation could be used to find the perimeter of the figure shown below?

   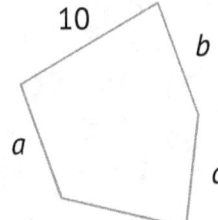

   A. $a + a + b + c = 10$
   B. $2a + b + c + 10 = P$
   C. $a + b + c + 10 = P$
   D. $a + b + c = 10$

   7.EE.4

3. Earl wants to earn enough money to purchase a bike that costs $515. For every lawn he mows he earns $25 and then gets a daily bonus of $15. What is the minimum number of lawns he would need to mow in 5 days to have enough money to buy the bike?

   A. 16
   B. 17
   C. 18
   D. 19

   7.EE.4

4. In order to be on the Honor Roll, Edie has to have an average that is more than 89. Her first 3 scores were 92.1, 84.7 and 90.3. Which inequality could be used to find what her 4th score, S, must be in order to earn Honor Roll?

   A. $89 < 92.1 + 84.7 + 90.3 + S$
   B. $\dfrac{92.1 + 84.7 + 90.3 + S}{4} > 89$
   C. $89 > 92.1 + 84.7 + 90.3 + S$
   D. $89 \times 4 < 92.1 + 84.7 + 90.3 - S$

   7.EE.4

5. The number of mosquitoes is expected to increase by 1.8% next month. If m represents the current number of mosquitoes, which expression represents the expected number of mosquitoes?

   A. $m + 0.018$
   B. $1 + 0.018m$
   C. $1.18m$
   D. $m + 0.018m$

   7.EE.2

6. Flynn has 12 dollars and he earns 8 dollars for every hour he works. Which equation shows how many dollars, D, that Flynn has after H hours?

   A. $D = 8H + 12$
   B. $D = 8H$
   C. $D = 8H - 12$
   D. $D = 12H + 8$

   7.EE.4

TIP of the DAY

When using inequality symbols, remember that greater than or less than means they do not HAVE to be less than a number, they can be equal to that number.

42

WEEK 6 : DAY 2

1. Which equation could be used to find the perimeter of the figure shown below?

   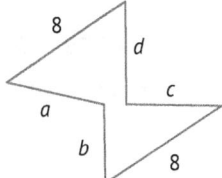

   A. $16 = a + b + c + d + 16$
   B. $P = a + b + c + d + 8$
   C. $16 = a + b + c + d$
   D. $P = a + b + c + d + 16$

   7.EE.4

2. If the perimeter of a rectangle is 120 cm and its length is 42 cm, which equation can be used to find the rectangle's width?

   A. $w = 120 - 42$
   B. $2w = \dfrac{120 - 42}{2}$
   C. $2w = 120 - 84$
   D. $w = 120 - 84$

   7.EE.4

3. Every minute Garret is able to run 124 meters. If he has already run 328 meters, what will his total distance be after 11 minutes?

   A. 1,692 meters
   B. 2,244 meters
   C. 3,674 meters
   D. 4,972 meters

   7.EE.4

4. Which expression is equivalent to $(14.5a + 6a - 3.4b) + (5.7b - 6.5a)$?

   A. $14a + 2.3b$
   B. $26.2a - 9.9b$
   C. $14a - 2.3b$
   D. $26.2a + 9.9b$

   7.EE.1

5. Erin earns \$13/hour but has to pay a \$14 internet fee for each day she works. Which equation shows how much money, m, Erin has after working h hours on 5 days?

   A. $m = 13h + 14$
   B. $m = 13h - 70$
   C. $h = 13m - 14$
   D. $m = 13h + 70$

   7.EE.4

6. What is the product of $\left(-\dfrac{2}{5}\right) \times \left(\dfrac{11}{20}\right)$?

   A. $\dfrac{3}{5}$
   B. $\dfrac{9}{15}$
   C. $-\dfrac{11}{50}$
   D. $-\dfrac{22}{25}$

   7.NS.2

TIP of the DAY

Sometimes you need a formula to solve an equation. Be sure to choose the correct one.

43

WEEK 6 : DAY 3

1. You are to solve the equation: $10r + 3 = -16$. What step should you take first?

   A. Add 16
   B. Subtract 3
   C. Multiply by $\frac{1}{10}$
   D. Divide by 10

   7.EE.4

2. If the perimeter of a rectangle is 480 in and its length is 215 inches, what is the rectangle's width?

   A. 25 inches
   B. 50 inches
   C. 265 inches
   D. 530 inches

   7.EE.4

3. The taxi charged $3.50 for a ride plus $1.75 per mile. How many complete miles could Gale travel for $30 if she left a $6 tip?

   A. 10
   B. 11
   C. 12
   D. 13

   7.EE.4

4. Felicity wants to purchase a sewing machine for $496. Each month she is able to save $29 for the purchase. If she has $211 already set aside, how many months will it take Felicity to save enough money to buy the sewing machine?

   A. 10   C. 12
   B. 11   D. 13

   7.EE.4

5. Foster owes his grandpa $16 but can earn $7/hour by doing yard work for him. If h is the number of hours Foster works, which equation can be used to find out how much money, m, Foster has after working h hours?

   A. $h = 7m + 16$ C. $m = 7h + 16$
   B. $h = 7m - 16$ D. $m = 7h - 16$

   7.EE.4

6. The regular cost of the car is c and there is $7\frac{3}{4}$% sales tax. What is the cost of the car including tax?

   A. $c + 0.775c$ C. $1 + 0.0775c$
   B. $1.0775c$ D. $c + 0.0775$

   7.EE2

TIP of the DAY

When solving equations, first try to isolate the term that contains the variable.

44

WEEK 6 : DAY 4

1. You are to solve the equation: $8r - 8 = 8$. What step should you take first?

   A. Add 8
   B. Subtract 8
   C. Multiply by 8
   D. Divide by 8

   7.EE.4

2. Florence wants to buy a car for $14,835. Each month she is able to save $96 for the purchase. If she has $12,674 already set aside, how many months will it take Florence to save enough money to buy the car?

   A. 20
   B. 21
   C. 22
   D. 23

   7.EE.4

3. If the perimeter of a rectangle is 396 cm and its length is 105 cm, which equation can be used to find the rectangle's width, w?

   A. $w = 396 - 210$
   B. $2w = 396 - 210$
   C. $2w = 396 - 105$
   D. $w = 396 - 105$

   7.EE.4

4. Elizabeth kept record of the temperature for 5 days. When she added the 5 temperatures together she got a sum of −1.8°F. She recorded these numbers: −11°F, −3.2°F, −5.8°F and 2.9°F but was missing 1 recording. What was the missing temperature?

   A. 15.3°F
   B. 20°F
   C. −15.3°F
   D. −20°F

   7.NS.1

5. Glen earns $21.07 per hour. Below you can see how many hours he worked last week. How much did Glen earn last week? Round to nearest cent.

Wednesday	$10\frac{1}{3}$
Thursday	12.4
Friday	$10\frac{1}{6}$

   A. $678.93
   B. $684.78
   C. $688.23
   D. $693.20

   7.EE.3

TIP of the DAY

When solving equations, remember to perform the operations on both sides of the equation. If you multiply one side of the equation by 5, you need to multiply the other side of the equation by 5 too.

WEEK 6 : DAY 5

ASSESSMENT

1. Which equation could be used to find the perimeter of the figure shown below?

   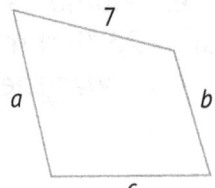

   A. $7 = a + b + c$
   B. $P - 7 = a + b + c$
   C. $P = a + b + c - 7$
   D. $7 = a + b + c - P$

   7.EE.4

2. You are to solve the equation: $-17 = 4x + 9$. What step should you take first?

   A. Add -17 and -9
   B. Subtract 9
   C. Multiply by $\frac{1}{4}$
   D. Divide by 4

   7.EE.4

3. If the perimeter of a rectangle is 390 inches and its length is 156 inches, what is the rectangle's width?

   A. 39 inches
   B. 78 inches
   C. 117 inches
   D. 234 inches

   7.EE.4

4. Gage earns $12.45 per hour. Below you can see how many hours he worked last week. How much did Gage earn last week?

Tuesday	$4\frac{1}{2}$
Thursday	$6\frac{1}{6}$
Friday	$10\frac{1}{3}$
Saturday	$9\frac{2}{5}$

   A. $361.05
   B. $377.86
   C. $378.48
   D. $382.17

   7.EE.3

5. If the number of chipmunks, c, is expected to increase by $4\frac{1}{2}$%, which expression represents the number of chipmunks after the increase?

   A. $1.045c$
   B. $1 + 0.45c$
   C. $c + 0.45$
   D. $c + 1.45c$

   7.EE.2

DAY 6 Challenge question

Gloria earns $8.95 for each wreath she sells at the flea market. She has to pay $25 to rent a space at the flea market. Write an equation that could be used to find Gloria's earnings, G, if she sells w wreaths.

7.EE.4

46

WEEK 7

VIDEO EXPLANATIONS ARGOPREP.COM

Week 7 provides practice using and finding unit rates and ratios. You will be able to find the constant of proportionality using graphs, tables and other visual representations.

You can find detailed video explanations of each problem in the book by visiting: ArgoPrep.com/ccm7

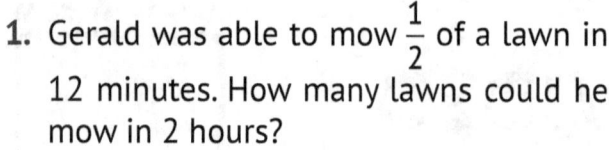

WEEK 7 : DAY 1

1. Gerald was able to mow $\frac{1}{2}$ of a lawn in 12 minutes. How many lawns could he mow in 2 hours?

   A. 3
   B. 4
   C. 5
   D. 6

   7.RP.1

2. Henley could draw 12 sketches in 5 hours. How many sketches could she draw in 3 hours?

   A. $1\frac{1}{4}$ sketches
   B. $5\frac{1}{4}$ sketches
   C. $6\frac{1}{5}$ sketches
   D. $7\frac{1}{5}$ sketches

   7.RP.1

3. Harold swam $6\frac{2}{5}$ km in 2 hours. How far could Harold swim in 5 hours?

   A. $3\frac{1}{5}$ km
   B. $12\frac{4}{5}$ km
   C. $15\frac{3}{5}$ km
   D. 16 km

   7.RP.1

4. If 4 bananas weigh $4\frac{4}{5}$ kilograms, how many kilograms would you expect 3 bananas to weigh?

   A. $\frac{2}{5}$
   B. $1\frac{3}{5}$
   C. $3\frac{3}{5}$
   D. 8

   7.RP.1

5. A load of fertilizer can be used on 390 yds² of land and weighs $1\frac{1}{2}$ tons. How many square yards could 1 ton of fertilizer cover?

   A. $\frac{1}{390}$
   B. 130
   C. 260
   D. 780

   7.RP.1

6. You are to solve the equation: $7t = 12 - 5t$. What step should you take first?

   A. Add $5t$
   B. Subtract $5t$
   C. Multiply by $\frac{1}{12}$
   D. Divide by 7

   7.EE.4

TIP of the DAY

When working with rates, finding the constant of proportionality first is always a good idea.

48

WEEK 7 : DAY 2

1. Herb was able to plant $2\frac{1}{3}$ rows of tomatoes in 15 minutes. How many rows could Herb plant in an hour?

   A. $8\frac{1}{3}$
   B. $9\frac{1}{3}$
   C. 10
   D. $11\frac{2}{3}$

   7.RP.1

2. Hailey was able to sew 3 dresses in $2\frac{1}{2}$ hours. How many dresses could Hailey sew in $7\frac{1}{2}$ hours?

   A. $5\frac{1}{2}$
   B. 6
   C. 9
   D. $9\frac{1}{2}$

   7.RP.1

3. If 5 bags of apples weigh $12\frac{1}{7}$ pounds, how many pounds would you expect 1 bag of apples to weigh?

   A. $2\frac{3}{7}$
   B. $3\frac{4}{7}$
   C. $4\frac{2}{7}$
   D. $5\frac{1}{7}$

   7.RP.1

4. Three pillowcases can be made with $1\frac{1}{2}$ yards of fabric. How many pillowcases can be made with $16\frac{1}{2}$ yards of fabric?

   A. 8
   B. 17
   C. 25
   D. 33

   7.RP.1

5. Heidi was able to walk $\frac{2}{3}$ of a mile in 12 minutes. How far could Heidi walk in 1 hour?

   A. $2\frac{2}{3}$
   B. $3\frac{1}{3}$
   C. $5\frac{1}{3}$
   D. 8

   7.RP.1

6. Each hour Hanna is able to run 4 kilometers. If she has already run 2 kilometers, what will her total distance be after 8 hours?

   A. 31 kilometers
   B. 32 kilometers
   C. 33 kilometers
   D. 34 kilometers

   7.EE.4

TIP of the DAY

To find the unit rate, find the number of "things" per unit (hour, minute, yard, row, etc.).

49

WEEK 7 : DAY 3

1. Ira used $\frac{1}{2}$ a gallon of paint to $\frac{3}{4}$ of his deck. How many gallons would it take to paint the entire deck?

   A. $\frac{1}{6}$
   B. $\frac{5}{6}$
   C. $\frac{1}{3}$
   D. $\frac{2}{3}$

   7.RP.1

2. Peaches cost $1.79 per pound. What equation is used to find C, the total cost for p pounds of peaches?

   A. C = 1.79p
   B. C = 1.79 + p
   C. C + 1.79 = p
   D. 1.79C = p

   7.RP.2

Use the 4 tables below to answer questions 3 – 5.

A.

x	y
2	4
3	6
4	8

B.

x	y
12	4
9	3
6	2

C.

x	y
0	0
1	1
2	2

D.

x	y
1	2
2	3
3	4

3. Which table has NO constant of proportionality?

   A. A
   B. B
   C. C
   D. D

   7.RP.2

4. Which table shows a constant of proportionality of 2?

   A. A
   B. B
   C. C
   D. D

   7.RP.2

5. Which table has a constant of proportionality of $\frac{1}{3}$?

   A. A
   B. B
   C. C
   D. D

   7.RP.2

TIP of the DAY

Pay attention to the variables and what they represent.

WEEK 7 : DAY 4

1. Chicken thighs cost $.68 per pound. What equation is used to find C, the total cost for *t* pounds of chicken?

   A. $t = 0.68c$
   B. $C = 0.68 + t$
   C. $C + 0.68 = t$
   D. $C = 0.68t$

   7.RP.2

2. Leather can be purchased for $8.21 per square yard. What equation is used to find C, the total cost for *L* square yards of leather?

   A. $C + 8.21 = L$
   B. $C = 8.21L$
   C. $C + L = 8.21$
   D. $L + 8.21 = C$

   7.RP.2

Please use the 4 tables below to answer questions 3 – 5.

A.

x	y
0	0
3	3
6	6

B.

x	y
3	9
5	12
7	15

C.

x	y
2	6
4	12
6	18

D.

x	y
5	2
10	4
15	6

3. Which table shows a constant of proportionality of 3?

   A. A
   B. B
   C. C
   D. D

   7.RP.2

4. What is the constant of proportionality for Table D?

   A. $\dfrac{1}{3}$
   B. $\dfrac{2}{5}$
   C. $\dfrac{5}{2}$
   D. 3

   7.RP.2

5. Which table does NOT have a constant of proportionality?

   A. A
   B. B
   C. C
   D. D

   7.RP.2

TIP of the DAY

The constant of proportionality, k, is found by $k = \dfrac{y}{x}$.

51

WEEK 7 : DAY 5

ASSESSMENT

1. Jenni bought 5 pounds of grapes for $7.40. If c represents the cost, in dollars, and g represents the pounds of grapes purchased, which equation best represents this relationship?

   A. $c = 1.48g$
   B. $c = 7.4g$
   C. $c = 5g$
   D. $c = 37g$

   7.RP.2

Use the tables below to answer questions 2 – 4.

A.

x	y
1	2
3	4
5	6

B.

x	y
3	1.5
7	3.5
11	5.5

C.

x	y
8	2
16	4
24	6

D.

x	y
3	12
5	20
7	28

2. Which table shows a constant of proportionality of 4?

   A. A
   B. B
   C. C
   D. D

   7.RP.2

3. What is the constant of proportionality for Table B?

   A. $\frac{1}{2}$
   B. $1\frac{1}{2}$
   C. 2
   D. 4

   7.RP.2

4. Which table does NOT have a constant of proportionality?

   A. A
   B. B
   C. C
   D. D

   7.RP.2

5. Carpet remnants are $5.08 per square yard. What equation is used to find C, the total cost for y square yards of carpet?

   A. $C = 5.08 + y$
   B. $C + 5.08 = y$
   C. $C = 5.08y$
   D. $5.08C = y$

   7.RP.2

DAY 6
Challenge question

If you know that the constant of proportionality is $\frac{2}{3}$ and you are told that $x = 6$, what is the value of y?

7.RP.2

52

WEEK 8

VIDEO EXPLANATIONS

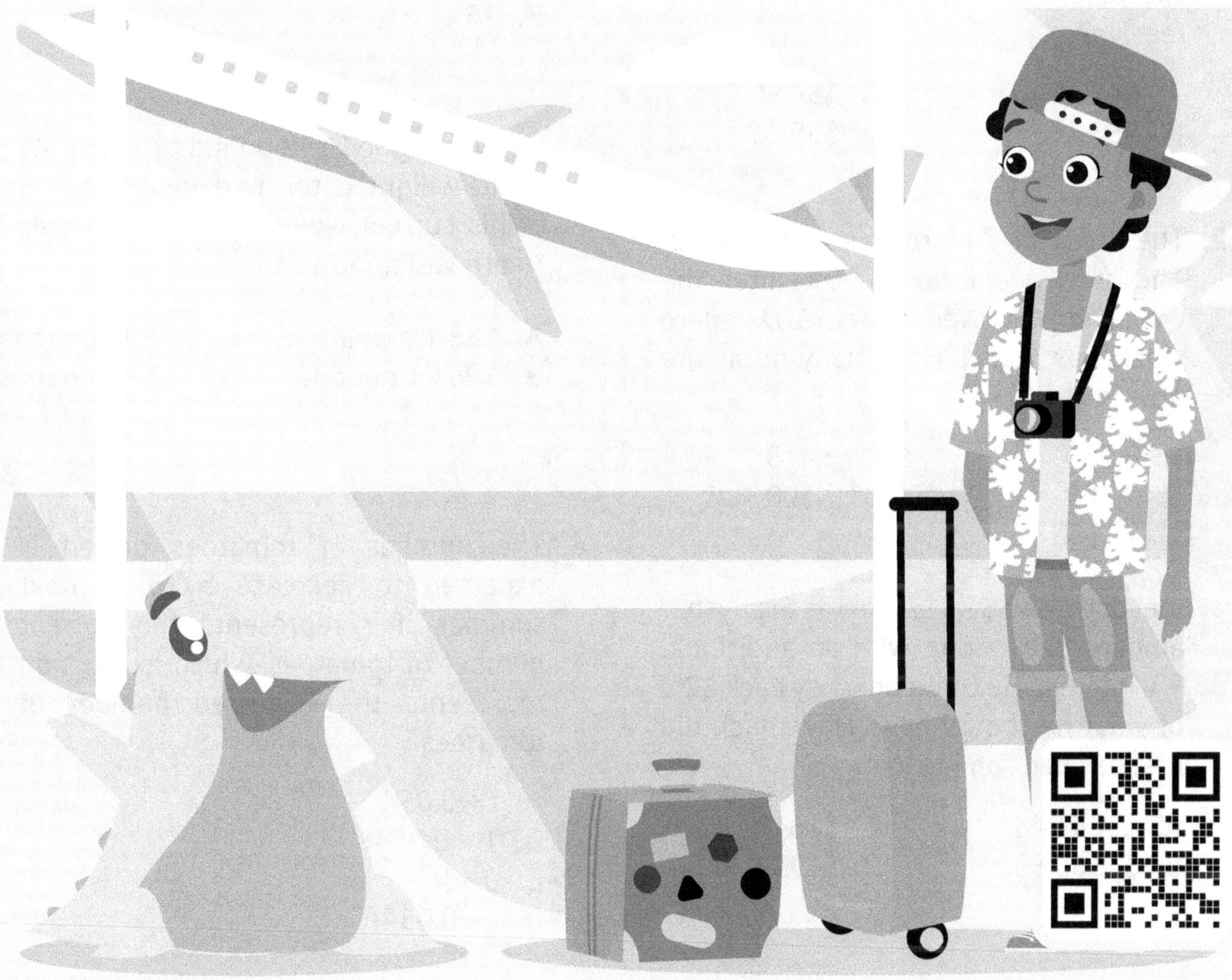

Week 8 gives lots of examples of percents and proportions as you find simple interest, taxes, discounts, markups and commissions. These topics are very relevant for people who shop, borrow money and/or work in sales.

You can find detailed video explanations of each problem in the book by visiting:
ArgoPrep.com/ccm7

WEEK 8 : DAY 1

1. Haven bought a pair of jeans that were regularly $79 but were discounted 25%. She decided to return them but she didn't have receipt. The store would only give her credit for 90% of the price she paid. How much credit did Haven receive?

   A. $48.60
   B. $53.33
   C. $54.90
   D. $59.25

   7.RP.3

2. The stock at Z-Mart was 2,500 items. The stock went down 10% after the weekend. On Wednesday, 10% more stock was added. How many items are now in stock?

   A. 2,250
   B. 2,300
   C. 2,475
   D. 2,500

   7.RP.3

3. Joel borrowed $1,512. He was to pay that amount back along with an additional 9% interest. He could only pay back 82% of what he should have. How much did Joel pay back on his loan?

   A. $1351.43
   B. $1360.80
   C. $1648.08
   D. $1944.73

   7.RP.3

4. Last month the Zimmer family had 20 chickens. This month they have 25. What is the percent increase from last month to this month?

   A. 80%
   B. 25%
   C. 20%
   D. 5%

   7.RP.3

5. Heath weighed 198 pounds. He lost 5% of his weight. Later he gained back 7% of his current weight. How much does Heath weigh now?

   A. 188.1 pounds
   B. 196.01 pounds
   C. 201.27 pounds
   D. 201.96 pounds

   7.RP.3

6. The number of tomatoes picked is expected to decrease by 5.4% next summer. If t represents the current number of tomatoes, which expression represents the expected number of tomatoes?

   A. $t + 0.054$
   B. $1 + 0.054t$
   C. $0.46t$
   D. $t - 0.054t$

   7.EE.2

TIP of the DAY

It is always important to ask yourself: "Percent of what?" The answer makes a difference.

54

WEEK 8 : DAY 2

1. The Bruins won 50 games last year and only 42 games this year. What is the percent decrease in the number of games the Bruins won last year compared to this year?

   A. 8%
   B. 16%
   C. 19%
   D. 84%

2. Drew made $18 per hour. Then he got a 10% raise. After cutbacks, he then had to reduce his hourly rate by 3%. What is his hourly rate after the cutbacks?

   A. $18.15
   B. $18.79
   C. $19.21
   D. $19.26

3. A pair of jeans normally sells for $112. They were on sale for 25% off the regular price on Black Friday. The next week the jeans were 15% more than the sales price. What is the new price of the jeans?

   A. $84.00
   B. $96.60
   C. $102.00
   D. $100.80

4. Calista had 24 pairs of socks before she went on vacation. After vacation she only had 18 pairs. What is the percent of decrease of socks from before until after vacation?

   A. 6%
   B. 18%
   C. 25%
   D. 33%

5. Irene's score on Test 1 was 120. Her score on Test 2 was 108. What is the percent decrease from Test 1 to Test 2?

   A. 10%
   B. 11%
   C. 12%
   D. 13%

6. What is the product of $\left(-\dfrac{4}{10}\right) \times \left(\dfrac{-8}{20}\right)$?

   A. $-\dfrac{4}{25}$
   B. $\dfrac{4}{25}$
   C. -1
   D. 1

TIP of the DAY: When looking at percentages, the percentage is based upon the original (or starting) number.

WEEK 8 : DAY 3

1. If you pay today, the camp costs $420. If you wait until tomorrow, the cost increases by 5%. What will the cost be tomorrow?

   A. $399
   B. $415
   C. $425
   D. $441

   7.EE.3

2. Donavan was used to making $12 per hour. He got a new job in which he made 8% more. After he got fired from that job he took another job where he made 3% more than his second job. How much did he make per hour at the third job?

   A. $12.57
   B. $12.96
   C. $13.35
   D. $13.58

   7.RP.3

3. What is the percent increase of people who saw the play on Monday night compared with those who saw the play on Saturday night?

   A. 10%
   B. 50%
   C. 100%
   D. 200%

   7.RP.3

4. What is the percent decrease from those who went on Friday night compared with those who went on Wednesday night?

   A. 40%
   B. 50%
   C. 67%
   D. 200%

   7.RP.3

The chart below shows the number of people who watched a play on different nights during the week.
Use the table below to answer questions 3 – 5.

Monday	Wednesday	Friday	Saturday
400	300	500	800

5. What is the percent increase of people who saw the play on Friday night compared with those who saw the play on Saturday night?

   A. 38%
   B. 40%
   C. 50%
   D. 60%

   7.RP.3

TIP of the DAY

Remember a decimal can be changed to a percent by moving the decimal 2 places.

WEEK 8 : DAY 4

1. The price of the dining room set was $1450. One of the chairs was broken so they discounted it 30%. They replaced the broken chair with a new one and increased the price by 25%. What is the new price?

   A. $1,015.00
   B. $1,268.75
   C. $1,377.50
   D. $1,522.50

   7.RP.3

2. Jorge's driving test score was a 76. After he retook the driving test his score was 88. What is the percent increase from the first test to the second test?

   A. 12.0%   C. 15.8%
   B. 13.6%   D. 16.4%

   7.RP.3

3. There are 3 sides to a triangle. The first side is 12 cm. The second side is 20% longer than the first side. The third side is 21% shorter than the second side. How long is the third side?

   A. 10.5 cm   C. 11.9 cm
   B. 11.4 cm   D. 14.4 cm

   7.RP.3

4. A shirt normally sells for $65. It was on sale for 45% off the regular price for 3 days. On the fourth day it increased by 10% more than the sales price. What is the new price?

   A. $35.75
   B. $36.35
   C. $38.73
   D. $39.33

   7.RP.3

5. A deposit for a trip is $986. If you pay today, you can receive a 10% discount. What will the deposit be if you pay today?

   A. $887.40
   B. $899.30
   C. $937.60
   D. $976.00

   7.RP.3

6. Evaluate: −102.3 + 15.8 − (−32) − 0.4

   A. − 150.5
   B. − 132.7
   C. − 118.9
   D. − 54.9

   7.NS.1

TIP of the DAY

Tomorrow when taking the assessment, remember to ask the question: Percent of what?

WEEK 8 : DAY 5

ASSESSMENT

The chart below shows the number of worms James caught on different days during the week. **Use the table below to answer questions 1 – 3.**

Monday	Wednesday	Friday	Saturday
50	36	45	10

1. What is the percent increase of worms James caught on Wednesday compared to the number he caught on Friday night?

   A. 9%
   B. 17%
   C. 25%
   D. 31%

   7.RP.3

2. What is the percent decrease in worms James caught on Monday compared to the number he caught on Saturday night?

   A. 20%
   B. 40%
   C. 50%
   D. 80%

   7.RP.3

3. What is the percent increase of worms James caught on Saturday compared to the number he caught on Wednesday night?

   A. 26%
   B. 72%
   C. 130%
   D. 260%

   7.RP.3

4. What is the decimal equivalent of $\frac{12}{15}$?

   A. 0.03
   B. 0.3
   C. 0.45
   D. 0.8

   7.NS.2

5. The perimeter of a rectangle is 77.4 feet. If the width is 12.9 feet, what is the length?

   A. 12.9 feet
   B. 25.8 feet
   C. 38.7 feet
   D. 51.6 feet

   7.EE.4

DAY 6
Challenge question

Hyatt scored an 80 on his first test and a 90 on his second test. Jensen scored an 88 on his first test and a 92 on his second test. Who had the largest percent of increase?

7.RP.3

WEEK 9

Statistics are the core of Week 9. You will practice finding and using random samples of a population. You will also begin to understand certain populations by gathering data and interpreting this data that reflects the given population.

You can find detailed video explanations of each problem in the book by visiting:
ArgoPrep.com/ccm7

WEEK 9 : DAY 1

1. The art teacher wants to know which art class 6th grade students are most likely to take. Which population would be the most representative?

   A. All of the 7th grade girls
   B. Every 5th sixth-grader in the attendance book
   C. All of the 6th grade boys
   D. 6th grade art students

   7.SP.1

2. The athletic department wants to know which sport is the most popular at the middle school. Which population would be the best group to ask?

   A. 15 boys and 15 girls from each grade in the middle school
   B. Every 10th eighth-grader
   C. Half of the 6th grade girls
   D. All of the 7th grade boys

   7.SP.1

3. A girls' teen magazine wants to know what articles its subscribers would like to read. Which population would be the best one to sample?

   A. The parents who purchase the magazine for their teens
   B. Girls who read the magazine in the checkout lane
   C. Brothers who have sisters that read the magazine
   D. Every 30th girl who has a subscription

   7.SP.1

4. There are 6 eighth-grade homerooms at Avon Middle School. If one of the homerooms is given a survey to answer, which statement best describes the scope of the survey?

   A. The results are representative of 8th graders across the school.
   B. The results are representative of 8th graders across the county.
   C. The results are representative of 8th graders across the state.
   D. The results are representative of 8th graders across the world.

   7.SP.1

Sampling groups should be representative of the given population.

60

WEEK 9 : DAY 2

1. The veterinarian wants to find out how much the pets in shelters weigh. Which sample would be the most representative?

   A. Weigh all the cats in the shelter
   B. Weigh every 10th pet in 20 shelters
   C. Weigh all the pets that were brought to the shelter last night
   D. Weigh every 5th dog in the shelter

   7.SP.1

2. The ETJ phone company from Ohio wants to know how many 7th graders in Ohio have cell phones. Which method would be the best way to survey a representative population?

   A. Call ETJ customers
   B. Call 7th grade students on their parents' landlines
   C. Send a survey in the mail to every 25th seventh-grader in Ohio
   D. Send a survey via email to every 7th grader in the United States

   7.SP.1

3. A mall wants to conduct a survey about its customers. Which sample would be the LEAST representative?

   A. Surveying every 6th person who walks out with a shopping bag
   B. Surveying every 8th person who enters the mall
   C. Surveying the shoppers in line at a checkout lane
   D. Surveying the Food Court workers

   7.SP.1

4. There are 586 seventh-grade homerooms in Pennsylvania. If the governor wants to know how many seventh-graders plan to attend college and he surveys 60 random homerooms, which statement best describes the scope of the survey?

   A. The results are representative of 7th graders across a school district.
   B. The results are representative of 7th graders across the county.
   C. The results are representative of 7th graders across the state.
   D. The results are representative of 7th graders across the world.

   7.SP.1

Sampling should be representative but still random.

WEEK 9 : DAY 3

1. Johann randomly picked 20% of the 8th graders to ask them their favorite sport. If 39 of the students said basketball, what is the most reasonable prediction of the number of 8th grade students who would pick basketball as their favorite sport?

   A. 8
   B. 20
   C. 160
   D. 200

   7.SP.2

2. If 25% of cheerleaders are surveyed and 170 of them say their favorite color is red, what is the most reasonable prediction of the number of cheerleaders who would pick red as their favorite color?

   A. 43
   B. 128
   C. 680
   D. 721

   7.SP.2

The chart below shows the results of a school survey to see who would be elected Student Body President. **Use the table below to answer questions 3 – 4.**

Candidate	Females who would vote for	Males who would vote for
Jeri	16	5
Jamaal	7	11
Jayda	10	10
Jaxon	9	15

3. Based on the survey, who would most likely become Student Body President?

   A. Jeri
   B. Jamaal
   C. Jayda
   D. Jaxon

   7.SP.2

4. Based on the survey, who would most likely receive the fewest votes?

   A. Jeri
   B. Jamaal
   C. Jayda
   D. Jaxon

   7.SP.2

TIP of the DAY

If 10% of a population is surveyed and responds a certain way, then the total number of people likely to respond the same way is about 10 times the survey's result.

62

WEEK 9 : DAY 4

1. When 25% of 18 year-olds were asked how many car accidents they had been in, 22 of them said more than 3. What is the most reasonable prediction of the number of 18 year-olds that have had more than 3 car accidents?

   A. 60
   B. 70
   C. 80
   D. 90

   7.SP.2

2. When 20% of soccer players were asked how many games they played last season, 34 of them said 15. What is the most reasonable prediction of the number of soccer players that played 15 games last season?

   A. 7
   B. 70
   C. 170
   D. 340

   7.SP.2

The chart below shows the results of a school survey to see which play students would like to see performed at their school. **Use the table below to answer questions 3 – 4.**

Plays	Females	Males
Sound of Music	18	2
Wizard of Oz	7	14
Narnia	14	13
The Secret Garden	15	4

3. Based on the survey, which play would most students want to see performed?

   A. Sound of Music
   B. Wizard of Oz
   C. Narnia
   D. The Secret Garden

   7.SP.2

4. Based on the survey, which play would the fewest number of students want to see performed?

   A. Sound of Music
   B. Wizard of Oz
   C. Narnia
   D. The Secret Garden

   7.SP.2

TIP of the DAY

If 20% of a population is sampled, only $\frac{1}{5}$ of the population was surveyed.

WEEK 9 : DAY 5

ASSESSMENT

Ten percent of the college campus was surveyed to find the students' favorite movie. The table below shows the number of students who voted for each movie. **Use this information to answer questions 1 – 4.**

Star Bride	21
Jason Burne	18
Ben Hurt	13
Fast & Angry	17
Cinderfella	19

1. Based on the survey, what is the most reasonable prediction of the number of all college students that would probably enjoy watching Star Bride the most?

   A. 21
   B. 31
   C. 210
   D. 231

   7.SP.2

2. Based on the survey, which movie would the fewest college students like to watch?

   A. Star Bride
   B. Jason Burne
   C. Ben Hurt
   D. Cinderfella

   7.SP.2

3. Based on the survey, what is the most reasonable prediction of the number of all college students that would probably enjoy watching Ben Hurt the most?

   A. 10
   B. 23
   C. 75
   D. 130

   7.SP.2

4. Based on the survey, which movie would most college students like to watch?

   A. Star Bride
   B. Jason Burne
   C. Ben Hurt
   D. Cinderfella

   7.SP.2

5. Which property is shown below?

   $$(12a - 15) = 3(4a - 5)$$

   A. Associative Property
   B. Commutative Property
   C. Distributive Property
   D. Inverse Property

   7.EE.1

DAY 6
Challenge question

In the movie table above, only ten percent of college students were surveyed. How many college students were there in total?

7.SP.2

WEEK 10

Now that you know and understand data sets, in Week 10 you will practice comparing and contrasting the information provided in data sets that may not look the same.

You can find detailed video explanations of each problem in the book by visiting: ArgoPrep.com/ccm7

WEEK 10 : DAY 1

Below is shown the runs scored by the Tigers and the Lions. **Use this information to answer questions 1 – 2.**

Runs scored by the Tigers   Runs scored by the Lions

1. What conclusion can you make about the data shown above?

   A. The Lions had a higher median score than the Tigers' median score.
   B. The Tigers had a higher mean than the Lions mean score.
   C. The Tigers had a greater range than the Lions.
   D. The Lions had a lower mean than the Tigers.

   7.SP.3

2. What is the difference between the medians of the 2 data sets?

   A. 1   C. 2
   B. $1\frac{1}{2}$ D. $2\frac{1}{2}$

   7.SP.3

Janine's scores are shown below. **Use the information to answer questions 3 – 4.**

| English | 72 | 88 | 90 | 79 | 85 |
| History | 94 | 80 | 92 | 86 | 88 |

3. What is the approximate difference between the ranges of the 2 class scores?

   A. 4   C. 14
   B. 8   D. 18

   7.SP.3

4. Which statement is true about Janine's English and history scores?

   A. Janine's history scores had a larger range.
   B. Janine's median score for history was larger than her median score for English.
   C. Janine's mean score for English was larger than her mean score for history.
   D. Janine's mean score for history was less than her mean score for English.

   7.SP.3

TIP of the DAY

Median is the middle number when the numbers are ranked from smallest to largest. For example, the median of 1, 4, 6, 7, 18, 20, 20 is 7.

WEEK 10 : DAY 2

The number of players that scored a certain number of points in 2 different games is shown below. **Use the information to answer questions 1 – 2.**

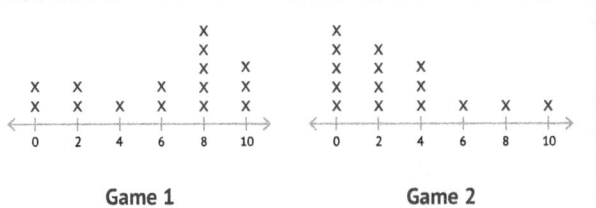

The heights of 10 students from one 4th grade class and one 5th grade class are shown below (in inches). **Use the information to answer questions 3 – 4.**

4th Grades Heights						5th Grades Heights				
4	7	8	9			4	8	9		
5	0	1	5	7	9	5	4	6	8	8
6	2	2				6	0	1	2	3

1. What is the difference in the ranges of the 2 data sets?

    A. 0   C. 4
    B. 2   D. 6

    7.SP.3

2. Which of the following statements is true regarding the 2 sets of data?

    A. The median for Game 2 is higher than the median for Game 1.
    B. The mean for Game 1 is less than the mean for Game 2.
    C. The range for Game 2 is greater than the range for Game 1.
    D. The Mean Absolute Deviation (MAD) is higher for Game 1 than for Game 2.

    7.SP.3

3. Using the information above, which statement is true?

    A. The 4th grade has a broader range than the 5th grade range.
    B. The 4th grade median is 5 less than the 5th grade median.
    C. The 4th grade mean is more than the 5th grade mean.
    D. The 5th grade has a broader range than the 4th grade range.

    7.SP.3

4. What is the difference between the means of the 2 data sets?

    A. 0
    B. 0.88
    C. 2.9
    D. 5

    7.SP.3

TIP of the DAY

The mean is another word for the average of a set of numbers.

67

WEEK 10 : DAY 3

The weights of 2 types of dogs are shown below (in pounds). **Use the information to answer questions 1 – 2.**

| Chihuahua | 4 | 4 | 5 | 7 | 8 | 9 | 12 |
| Labrador | 45 | 52 | 56 | 59 | 61 | 62 | 62 |

1. What is the difference between the ranges of the two dogs?

   A. 6
   B. 8
   C. 9
   D. 11

   7.SP.3

2. Which statement is true about the weights of the Chihuahuas and the Labrador Retrievers?

   A. The mean weight of the Labrador Retrievers is about 8 times the weight of the Chihuahas.
   B. The mean weight of the Chihuahuas is about $\frac{1}{4}$ of the mean weight of the Labrador Retrievers.
   C. The median weight of the Chihuahuas is about $\frac{1}{4}$ of the mean weight of the Labrador Retrievers.
   D. The range is the same for both types of dogs.

   7.SP.3

The number of times Jeffrey and Jonah drove to the store in a week over 12 weeks is shown below. **Use the information to answer questions 3 – 4.**

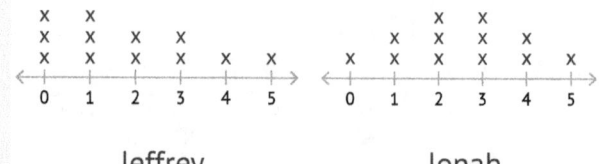

Jeffrey   Jonah

3. Which statement is true about the data sets showing Jeffrey and Jonah's trips to the store?

   A. The difference between the sets' means is 0.75.
   B. The medians of the 2 data sets have a difference of exactly 1.0.
   C. Jeffrey has a larger range in his data than Jonah.
   D. Jonah has a larger range in his data than Jeffrey.

   7.SP.3

4. Which number is closest to the difference between the MADs of the 2 data sets?

   A. 0.17
   B. 0.67
   C. 1.16
   D. 1.3

   7.SP.3

TIP of the DAY

MAD stands for the Mean Absolute Deviation.

WEEK 10 : DAY 4

The amount of hair (in inches) that Kiera and Jackie had trimmed is shown below. **Use this information to answer questions 1 – 4.**

Kiera	0.6	0.75	1.4	1.5	3.25
Jackie	0.8	1.25	1.5	2.2	2.5

1. What is the mean of the data set that shows the amount of hair that Kiera had trimmed?

   A. 1.4
   B. 1.5
   C. 1.65
   D. 1.7

   7.SP.3

2. What is the median of the data set that shows the amount of hair that Jackie had trimmed?

   A. 1.4
   B. 1.5
   C. 1.65
   D. 1.7

   7.SP.3

3. Which number is the largest?

   A. The difference between the 2 MADs
   B. The difference between the 2 means
   C. The difference between the 2 medians
   D. The difference between the 2 ranges

   7.SP.3

4. Which number is the smallest?

   A. The difference between the 2 MADs
   B. The difference between the 2 means
   C. The difference between the 2 medians
   D. The difference between the 2 ranges

   7.SP.3

5. Kaylee could knit 15 scarves in 7.5 hours. How many scarves could she knit in 3.25 hours?

   A. $6\frac{1}{4}$ scarves
   B. $6\frac{1}{2}$ scarves
   C. $6\frac{3}{4}$ scarves
   D. $6\frac{7}{8}$ scarves

   7.RP.1

6. A deposit for a concert is $42. If you pay today, you can receive a 20% discount. What will the deposit be if you pay today?

   A. $50.40
   B. $37.80
   C. $33.60
   D. $29.40

   7.RP.3

TIP of the DAY

Tomorrow when taking the assessment, remember the difference between range, median, mean and Mean Absolute Deviation (MAD).

WEEK 10 : DAY 5

ASSESSMENT

There were 2 groups of runners, Group A and Group B. The distance the runners ran is shown below (in km). **Use the information from the data sets to answer questions 1 - 4.**

A	Distance Run (km)				
0	8	8	9		
1	1	2	2	4	5	5	8
2	1	1	3	6	7
3	0	3	4	4	5

B	Distance Run (km)						
0	1	1	2	4	7	7	
1	2	3	3	6	8	9	
2	3	5	5	6	7	8	9
3	0						

1. What is the difference in the ranges of the 2 sets of data?

   A. 2
   B. 4
   C. 5
   D. 7
   7.SP.3

2. What is the difference in the means of the 2 sets of data?

   A. 2
   B. 4
   C. 5
   D. 7
   7.SP.3

3. What is the difference in the MADs between the 2 data sets?

   A. 0.6
   B. 2.5
   C. 6.0
   D. 16.8
   7.SP.3

4. Which statement is true about the 2 data sets?

   A. The range for Group A is larger than the range for Group B.
   B. The mean of Group A is 16.3.
   C. The difference between the 2 groups' medians is 2.5.
   D. The MAD for Group B is 8.015.
   7.SP.3

The chart below shows the number of fish Kurt caught on different days during the week. **Use the table below to answer questions 5 – 6.**

Wednesday	Friday	Saturday	Sunday
25	12	20	10

5. What is the percent decrease of fish Kurt caught on Wednesday compared to the number he caught on Saturday night?

   A. 5%
   B. 10%
   C. 20%
   D. 25%
   7.RP.3

6. What is the percent increase in fish Kurt caught on Sunday compared to the number he caught on Friday night?

   A. 5%
   B. 17%
   C. 20%
   D. 25%
   7.RP.3

DAY 6
Challenge question

Forty percent of baseball players were asked how many home runs they had hit. Fifty-six players said they had hit more than 10 home runs. Using this information, what is a reasonable number that indicates how many baseball players hit more than 10 home runs?

7.SP.2

WEEK 11

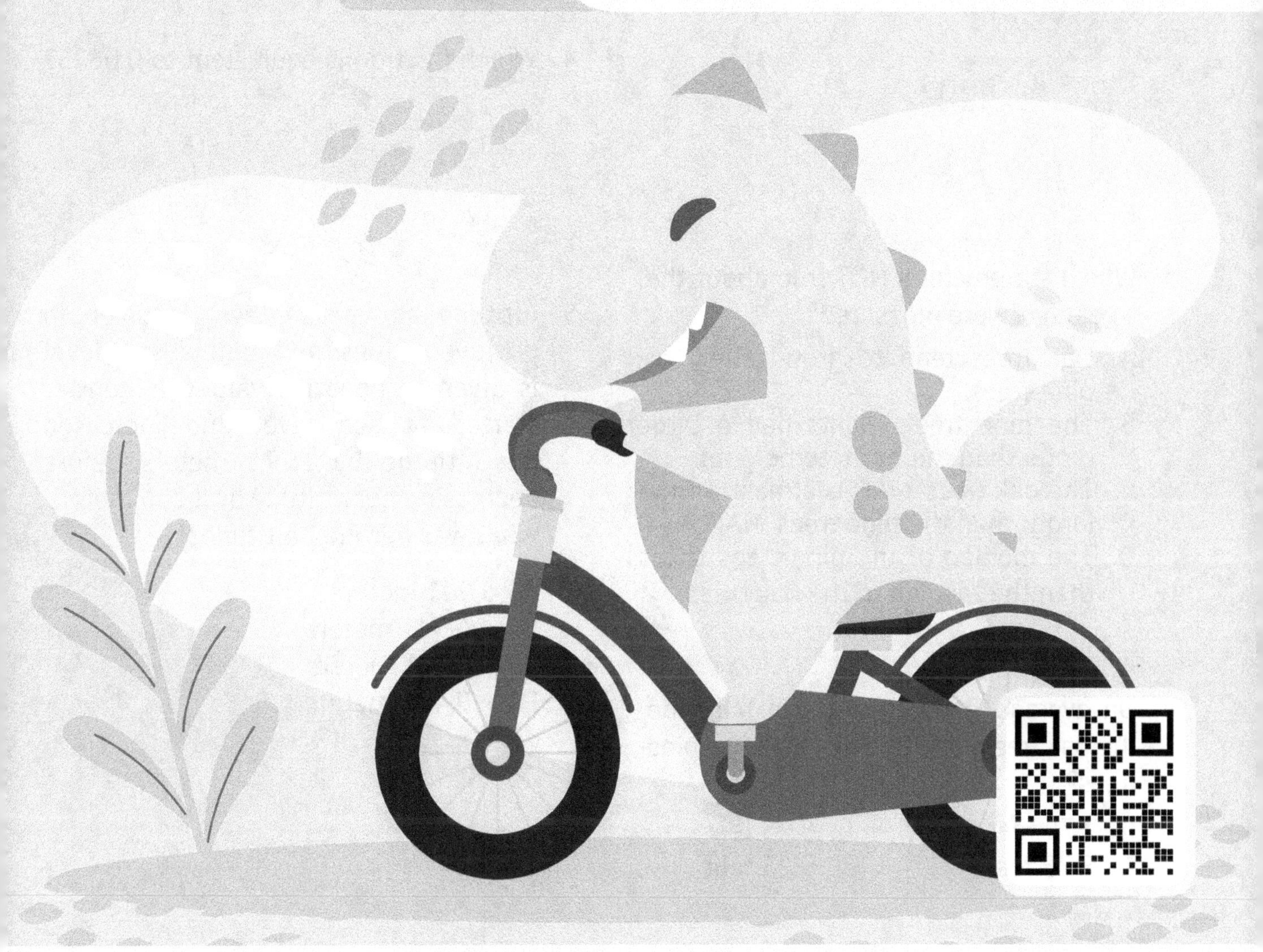

Further building on what you've learned about data, Week 11 lets you use the data sets to find measures of center and measures of variability. These measures are then used to infer how a population might respond to a given scenario.

You can find detailed video explanations of each problem in the book by visiting:
ArgoPrep.com/ccm7

WEEK 11 : DAY 1

Below are some measurements that were taken by a forest ranger. He measured 2 types of trees and charted the information. **Use the table below to answer questions 1 – 3.**

Number	Pine Height (feet)	Oak Height (feet)
1	22	32
2	19	25
3	18	38
4	23	22

1. Which statement is NOT true about the trees that were measured?
   A. Oak trees tend to grow taller than pine trees.
   B. The pine tree heights had a larger range than the oak tree heights.
   C. The oak trees' MAD is almost 3 times larger than the pine trees' MAD.
   D. The median of the pine trees is less than the median of the oak trees.

   7.SP.4

2. On average, about how much taller do the oak trees tend to grow than the pine trees?
   A. 7.75 feet   C. 8.75 feet
   B. 8.25 feet   D. 9.25 feet

   7.SP.4

3. What is the difference between the medians of the 2 data sets?
   A. 8 feet   C. 10 feet
   B. 9 feet   D. 11 feet

   7.SP.4

4. Which fraction is equivalent to 0.0625?
   A. $\dfrac{1}{8}$ C. $\dfrac{1}{16}$
   B. $\dfrac{1}{12}$ D. $\dfrac{1}{18}$

   7.NS.2

5. Altitude above sea level is given in positive values and below sea level is given in negative values. If Kentley started at sea level and increased her altitude by 1,275 meters before decreasing her altitude by 8,216 meters, what was her final altitude?
   A. 6,941 meters
   B. – 6,941 meters
   C. + 9,491 meters
   D. – 9,491 meters

   7.NS.1

TIP of the DAY

Study data sets to understand the information presented.

72

WEEK 11 : DAY 2

Below is a data set about the scores of 2 science classes. **Use the information to answer questions 1 – 4.**

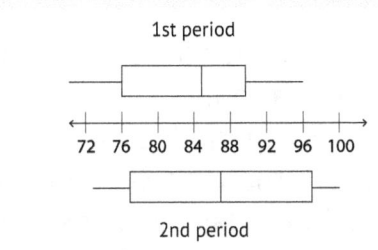

1. Which is most likely the range for the 1st period class?

   A. 5
   B. 14
   C. 20
   D. 27

   7.SP.4

2. What is the median score for 2nd period?

   A. 20
   B. 85
   C. 87
   D. 100

   7.SP.4

3. Which statement is true about the science scores?

   A. The interquartile range is the same for both periods.
   B. Second period has a higher median than first period.
   C. First period has a higher median than second period.
   D. The highest score in 1st period was a 90.

   7.SP.4

4. Which statement is NOT true about the science scores?

   A. The lowest score in first period was a 73.
   B. The interquartile range is larger for second period than it is for first period.
   C. The highest score in first period was a 96.
   D. First period has a lower mean than second period.

   7.SP.4

5. Liam's bicycle tire had a leak. It originally held 18 pounds of pressure but was losing 1.2 pounds of pressure each hour. How many pounds of pressure would remain after 5 hours?

   A. 11.8 pounds
   B. 12.0 pounds
   C. 13.2 pounds
   D. 16.8 pounds

   7.EE.3

6. Which expression is equivalent to:

   $(g + 4g - 5) - (4 - 10 - 3g)$

   A. $8g + 1$
   B. $8g - 19$
   C. $2g + 1$
   D. $2g - 19$

   7.EE.1

Mean is the mathematical term meaning average.

73

WEEK 11 : DAY 3

Below are the scores for 2 classes that took a math test. **Use the information provided to answer questions 1 – 4.**

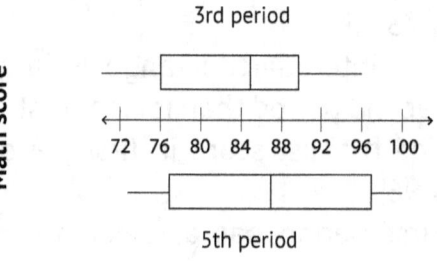

3. Which statement is NOT true for the 2 data sets?

   A. The range for 5th period is twice that of 3rd period.
   B. The 5th period class had a higher median than the 3rd period class.
   C. The interquartile range was smaller for the 3rd period class.
   D. The 3rd period class had a lower median than the 5th period class.

   7.SP.4

1. What is most likely the interquartile range for 3rd period?

   A. 2 C. 13
   B. 7 D. 20

   7.SP.4

4. What is most likely the difference between the medians of the 2 data sets?

   A. 2 C. 9
   B. 5 D. 13

   7.SP.4

2. Which statement is true about the 2 math classes?

   A. The 5th period class had a lower median score.
   B. The 5th period class had a range of 12.
   C. The 3rd period class had a range of 7.
   D. The 3rd period class had a lower median score.

   7.SP.4

5. The current taxes, t, on a car are expected to rise 9% over the next few years. What will the taxes be after that increase?

   A. $t + 0.9$
   B. $t + 0.09t$
   C. $1.9t$
   D. $t + 0.09$

   7.EE.2

TIP of the DAY

When studying sets of data, make sure you understand the information being presented before solving.

WEEK 11 : DAY 4

Below are some measurements that were taken by a horticulturalist, someone who studies plants. He measured 2 types of flowers and charted the information. **Use the table below to answer questions 1 – 4.**

Number	Daisy Height (cm)	Tulip Height (cm)
1	92	88
2	87	79
3	80	92
4	93	78
5	84	86

1. Which statement is true about the 2 sets of data?

    A. The tulips have a greater range.
    B. The tulips have a greater mean.
    C. The daisies have a greater MAD.
    D. The daisies have a lower median.

    7.SP.4

2. What is the difference between the Mean Absolute Deviation (MAD) of the 2 data sets?

    A. 64 C. 0.64
    B. 6.4 D. 0.064

    7.SP.4

3. What is the difference between the data sets' medians?

    A. 1 C. 2
    B. 1.6 D. 2.6

    7.SP.4

4. What is the difference between the data sets' ranges?

    A. 1 C. 2
    B. 1.6 D. 2.6

    7.SP.4

5. Below are some transactions that Kitty made with her bank account.

Deposits	Withdrawals
39.63	649.02
821.45	495.30

    If Kitty's account had $175 before any deposits or withdrawals, what was her final balance?

    A. – $108.24
    B. – $281.49
    C. $284.99
    D. $458.24

    7.NS.1

TIP of the DAY

If there is an even number of pieces of data, to find the median you find the average of the 2 middle numbers.

75

WEEK 11 : DAY 5

ASSESSMENT

One month Mark measured the rainfall each day. The data is shown below.
Use the information given to answer questions 1 – 4.

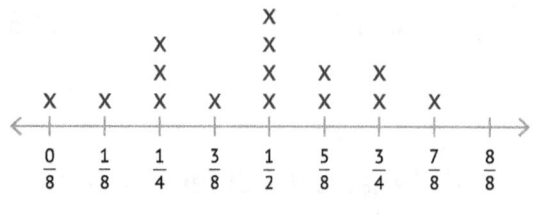

Days 1 - 15

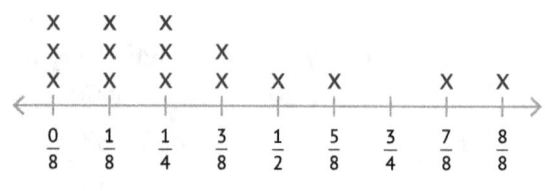

Days 16 - 30

1. Which statement is true about the 2 data sets that recorded the rainfall?

    A. Days 16 – 30 have a smaller range.
    B. Days 16 – 30 have a larger median.
    C. Days 1 – 15 have a smaller mean.
    D. Days 1 – 15 have a smaller range.

    7.SP.4

2. What is the difference between the 2 ranges of data?

    A. 0.0625
    B. 0.125
    C. 0.25
    D. 0.375

    7.SP.4

3. Which statement is true about the 2 sets of data?

    A. It is more likely to rain on the first 15 days of the month.
    B. It is more likely to rain on the last 15 days of the month.
    C. It is more likely to be drier on the first 15 days of the month.
    D. It is more likely to have a 0 inch day during the first 15 days of the month.

    7.SP.4

4. What is the difference between the medians of the 2 sets of data?

    A. 0.0625   C. 0.25
    B. 0.125   D. 0.375

    7.SP.4

DAY 6
Challenge question

Using the rainfall data shown for numbers 1 – 4, what is the median for BOTH data sets combined?

7.SP.4

Are you interested in odds? If so, you will find Week 12 fun! This week you will be asked to use frequency to understand and approximate chance events by predicting and observing outcomes.

You can find detailed video explanations of each problem in the book by visiting: ArgoPrep.com/ccm7

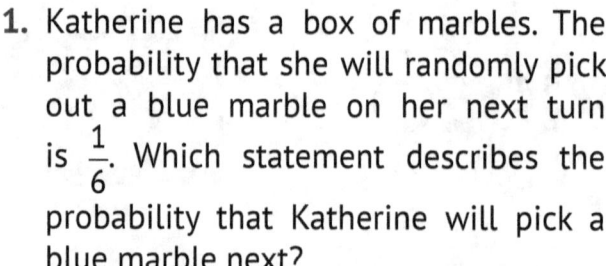

1. Katherine has a box of marbles. The probability that she will randomly pick out a blue marble on her next turn is $\frac{1}{6}$. Which statement describes the probability that Katherine will pick a blue marble next?

    A. likely
    B. certain
    C. unlikely
    D. impossible

2. Lucas is spinning a spinner. The probability that the spinner will land on 4 on his next turn is $\frac{1}{4}$. Which statement describes the probability that Lucas' next spin will be a 4?

    A. likely
    B. certain
    C. unlikely
    D. impossible

3. Penelope the Pig is pregnant. Which statement describes the probability that Penelope will give birth to a pig?

    A. likely
    B. certain
    C. unlikely
    D. impossible

4. Louis has a bag of stones. The probability that he will pick a marble is $\frac{0}{12}$. Which statement describes the probability that Louis will randomly select a marble?

    A. likely
    B. certain
    C. unlikely
    D. impossible

5. Leia is spinning a spinner. The probability that the spinner will land on 9 on her next turn is $\frac{3}{4}$. Which statement describes the probability that Leia's next spin will be a 9?

    A. likely
    B. certain
    C. unlikely
    D. impossible

6. Levi is kicking the ball into the goal. The probability that he will make the shot is $\frac{2}{3}$. Which statement describes the probability that Levi will score a goal?

    A. likely
    B. certain
    C. unlikely
    D. impossible

TIP of the DAY

An event that has a probability of 0.5 or $\frac{1}{2}$ is neither a likely nor an unlikely event.

78

WEEK 12 : DAY 2

1. Lara is shooting baskets. The probability that she will make the shot is $\frac{4}{5}$. Which statement describes the probability that Lara will make a basket?
   A. likely
   B. certain
   C. unlikely
   D. impossible
   7.SP.5

2. Angelo is choosing coins. There are 10 dimes, 5 nickels and 12 pennies to choose. Which statement describes the probability that Angelo will pick a coin?
   A. likely
   B. certain
   C. unlikely
   D. impossible
   7.SP.5

3. Klein has a pouch of stones. The probability that he will randomly pick out a smooth stone on his next turn is $\frac{2}{9}$. Which statement describes the probability that Klein will pick a smooth stone next?
   A. likely
   B. certain
   C. unlikely
   D. impossible
   7.SP.5

4. Dixie the Dog is pregnant. Which statement describes the probability that Dixie will give birth to a hippopotamus?
   A. likely
   B. certain
   C. unlikely
   D. impossible
   7.SP.5

5. The probability of Karin choosing 2 cards that equal a number greater than 3 is $\frac{9}{10}$. Which statement describes the probability that Karin will choose 2 cards that are greater than 3?
   A. likely
   B. certain
   C. unlikely
   D. impossible
   7.SP.5

6. Lisa is spinning a spinner. The probability that the spinner will land on a number on her next turn is $\frac{5}{5}$. Which statement describes the probability that Lisa's next spin will be a number?
   A. likely
   B. certain
   C. unlikely
   D. impossible
   7.SP.5

A certain event is one in which the desired outcome WILL happen.

WEEK 12 : DAY 3

Below is a game board where players are to "call" a number and/or a color. If the quarter lands on a square that the player "called", they win a point. **Use the picture below to answer questions 1 – 2.**

1	2	3	4
5	6	7	8

1. Maribel called a blue 2. What is the probability that Maribel will get a point?

    A. $\frac{0}{8}$ 　　　C. $\frac{3}{8}$

    B. $\frac{1}{8}$ 　　　D. $\frac{4}{8}$

2. Manny called an orange square. What is the probability that Manny will get a point?

    A. $\frac{1}{8}$ 　　　C. $\frac{3}{8}$

    B. $\frac{2}{8}$ 　　　D. $\frac{5}{8}$

    7.SP.6

3. If the probability of Kylie drawing a white sock from the laundry is $\frac{1}{5}$ and she randomly draws 1 sock at a time and replaces it, how many times would you expect Kylie to get a white sock if she tries 255 times?

    A. 24 　　　C. 51
    B. 35 　　　D. 62

    7.SP.6

4. Which fraction shows the probability that Michael will pick an ace from a standard 52-card deck?

    A. $\frac{1}{4}$ 　　　C. $\frac{1}{26}$

    B. $\frac{1}{13}$ 　　　D. $\frac{1}{52}$

    7.SP.6

5. Michelle has a jewelry box that contains 12 rubies, 4 sapphires, and 5 diamonds. Which statement describes the probability that Michelle will randomly pick a sapphire?

    A. likely
    B. certain
    C. unlikely
    D. impossible

    7.SP.5

TIP of the DAY

An impossible event is one in which the desired outcome can not possibly happen.

80

WEEK 12 : DAY 4

1. Looking at the game board below, what is the probability of landing on a purple square?

   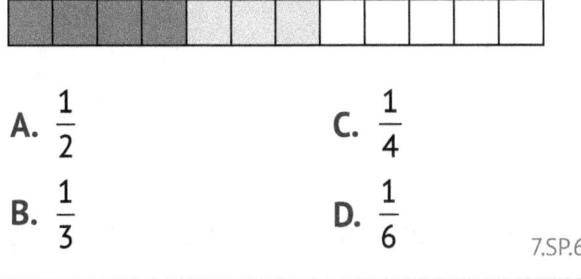

   A. $\frac{1}{2}$ C. $\frac{1}{4}$

   B. $\frac{1}{3}$ D. $\frac{1}{6}$

   7.SP.6

2. Which fraction shows the probability that Malia will roll a 2 on a fair die?

   A. $\frac{1}{2}$ C. $\frac{1}{4}$

   B. $\frac{1}{3}$ D. $\frac{1}{6}$

   7.SP.6

3. Which fraction shows the probability that Joey will pick a red card from a standard 52-card deck?

   A. $\frac{1}{2}$ C. $\frac{1}{8}$

   B. $\frac{1}{4}$ D. $\frac{1}{13}$

   7.SP.6

4. If the probability of Morgan drawing a red marble from a bag is $\frac{1}{8}$ and she draws 1 marble at a time and replaces it, how many times would you expect Morgan to get a red marble if she tries 200 times?

   A. 18
   B. 25
   C. 37
   D. 49

   7.SP.6

5. Which fraction shows the probability that Matthew will roll an even number on a fair die?

   A. $\frac{1}{2}$ C. $\frac{1}{4}$

   B. $\frac{1}{3}$ D. $\frac{1}{6}$

   7.SP.6

6. Which fraction shows the probability that Jaquis will pick a club from a standard 52-card deck?

   A. $\frac{1}{4}$ C. $\frac{1}{26}$

   B. $\frac{1}{13}$ D. $\frac{1}{52}$

   7.SP.6

TIP of the DAY

If the probability of an event is 1 in 8, it is said to have a probability of $\frac{1}{8}$ or 0.125.

WEEK 12 : DAY 5

ASSESSMENT

Below is a game board where players are to "call" a number and/or a color. If the quarter lands on a square that the player "called", they win a point. **Use the picture below to answer questions 1 – 2.**

1	2	3	4
5	6	7	8

1. What is the probability that a player would land on a green square?

   A. $\frac{1}{8}$

   B. $\frac{5}{8}$

   C. $\frac{1}{4}$

   D. $\frac{1}{2}$

   7.SP.6

2. What is the probability that a player would land on a square with an even number?

   A. $\frac{1}{8}$

   B. $\frac{5}{8}$

   C. $\frac{1}{4}$

   D. $\frac{1}{2}$

   7.SP.6

3. What is the probability that Monika will roll an 8 on a fair die?

   A. 0

   B. $\frac{1}{5}$

   C. $\frac{1}{6}$

   D. 1

   7.SP.6

4. If the probability of Mustafa drawing a flat stone from a bag is $\frac{1}{9}$. If he draws 1 stone at a time and replaces it, how many times would you expect Mustafa to get a flat stone if he tries 306 times?

   A. 34

   B. 45

   C. 53

   D. 66

   7.SP.6

5. You are to solve the equation: $5x = 15x + 22$. What step should you take first?

   A. Add $15x$

   B. Subtract $15x$

   C. Multiply by $\frac{1}{15}$

   D. Divide by 5

   7.EE.4

DAY 6
Challenge question

What is the probability that a person could flip a fair coin three times and get three tails?

7.SP.6

WEEK 13

VIDEO EXPLANATIONS — ARGOPREP.COM

Now that you understand a little bit more about probability and the likelihood of certain events, you can begin to create your own probability models using information you have been given.

You can find detailed video explanations of each problem in the book by visiting:
ArgoPrep.com/ccm7

WEEK 13 : DAY 1

There are 40 marbles in a bag and the number of each color is shown below. **Use the table below to answer questions 1 – 2.**

Color	Number
Blue	7
Red	10
Green	12
Yellow	8
Silver	3

1. Based on the data, what is the probability that Dax will draw out a green marble?

   A. $\frac{1}{4}$ C. $\frac{3}{10}$

   B. $\frac{1}{5}$ D. $\frac{3}{40}$

   7.SP.7

2. Based on the data, what is the probability that Noelle will draw out a red marble?

   A. $\frac{1}{4}$ C. $\frac{3}{10}$

   B. $\frac{1}{5}$ D. $\frac{3}{40}$

   7.SP.7

Noah had 25 golf balls in his golf bag. Eighteen of the balls were white and the rest were yellow. Five of the yellow golf balls had dots on them. **Use this information to answer questions 3 – 4.**

3. Based on the data, what is the probability that Noah will draw out a golf ball that contains a dot?

   A. 0.04   C. 0.25

   B. 0.2   D. 0.28

   7.SP.7

4. Based on the data, what is the probability that Noah will draw out a golf ball that does NOT contain a dot?

   A. 0.5   C. 0.8

   B. 0.72   D. 0.82

   7.SP.7

5. Neveah kept track of the temperature for several weeks. Her results are shown below. If her temperatures had a sum of -36.7°, what is the missing temperature?

Number of Days	Temperature
9	−1.5°F
6	3.2°F
5	−12°F
2	5.4°F
1	?

   A. −31.8°F

   B. −4.9°F

   C. 5.1°F

   D. 6.8°F

   7.NS.3

TIP of the DAY

Probability models can be used to find the probability (or likelihood) of a specific event happening.

WEEK 13 : DAY 2

There are 50 tokens in a box and the number of each color is shown below. **Use the table below to answer questions 1 – 4.**

Color	Number
White	12
Purple	9
Orange	10
Pink	11
Black	8

1. Based on the data, what is the probability that Celia will draw out a pink token?

   A. $\dfrac{1}{5}$ C. $\dfrac{6}{25}$

   B. $\dfrac{4}{25}$ D. $\dfrac{11}{50}$

   7.SP.7

2. Based on the data, what is the probability that Moe will draw out an orange token?

   A. $\dfrac{1}{5}$ C. $\dfrac{6}{25}$

   B. $\dfrac{4}{25}$ D. $\dfrac{11}{50}$

   7.SP.7

3. Based on the data, what is the probability that Maurice will draw out either a white OR a black token?

   A. $\dfrac{2}{5}$ C. $\dfrac{6}{25}$

   B. $\dfrac{4}{25}$ D. $\dfrac{10}{50}$

   7.SP.7

4. Based on the data, what is the probability that Melanie will draw out either a purple OR a pink token?

   A. $\dfrac{2}{5}$ C. $\dfrac{9}{50}$

   B. $\dfrac{1}{25}$ D. $\dfrac{11}{50}$

   7.SP.7

5. What is the decimal equivalent of $\dfrac{5}{12}$ rounded to the nearest thousandth?

   A. 0.378
   B. 0.417
   C. 0.486
   D. 0.512

   7.NS.2

TIP of the DAY

An impossible event has a probability of 0.

85

WEEK 13 : DAY 3

There are 4 students running for Class President. Fifty students were polled and their votes are shown below. **Use the table below to answer questions 1 – 4.**

Students	Number
Nicholas	14
Marissa	11
Oliver	10
Penelope	15

1. Based on the data, what is the probability that Penelope will win the election?

   A. $\frac{1}{5}$ C. $\frac{7}{25}$

   B. $\frac{3}{10}$ D. $\frac{11}{50}$

   7.SP.7

2. Based on the data, what is the probability that Nicholas will win the election?

   A. $\frac{1}{5}$ C. $\frac{7}{25}$

   B. $\frac{3}{10}$ D. $\frac{11}{50}$

   7.SP.7

3. Based on the data, what is the probability that a girl will win the election?

   A. $\frac{1}{2}$ C. $\frac{12}{25}$

   B. $\frac{3}{5}$ D. $\frac{13}{25}$

   7.SP.7

4. Based on the data, what is the probability that a boy will win the election?

   A. $\frac{1}{2}$ C. $\frac{12}{25}$

   B. $\frac{3}{5}$ D. $\frac{13}{25}$

   7.SP.7

5. If 20% of likely voters are surveyed and 210 of them say they would most likely vote for the tallest candidate for the office of City Painter, what is the most reasonable prediction of the number of voters who would choose the tallest candidate for City Painter?

   A. 840
   B. 1,050
   C. 1,570
   D. 1,890

   7.SP.2

TIP of the DAY

Probability does not guarantee an outcome, it only states what the likelihood of a particular event is.

WEEK 13 : DAY 4

There is a deck of cards and the number and type of card are shown below. **Use the table below to answer questions 1 – 4.**

Card	Number
Go Back	15
Draw One	8
Go Again	10
Skip Neighbor	12
Lose a Turn	15

1. Based on the data, what is the probability that a player would draw a Go Again card?

   A. $\dfrac{1}{4}$ C. $\dfrac{1}{6}$

   B. $\dfrac{1}{5}$ D. $\dfrac{2}{25}$

2. Based on the data, what is the probability that a player would draw a Skip Neighbor card?

   A. $\dfrac{1}{4}$ C. $\dfrac{1}{6}$

   B. $\dfrac{1}{5}$ D. $\dfrac{2}{25}$

   7.SP.7

3. Based on the data, what is the probability that a player would draw a Draw One card?

   A. $\dfrac{1}{4}$ C. $\dfrac{1}{6}$

   B. $\dfrac{1}{5}$ D. $\dfrac{2}{15}$

   7.SP.7

4. Based on the data, what is the probability that a player would NOT draw a Lose a Turn card?

   A. $\dfrac{3}{4}$ C. $\dfrac{5}{6}$

   B. $\dfrac{4}{5}$ D. $\dfrac{13}{15}$

   7.SP.7

5. The number of voters is expected to increase by 7.3% next election. If v represents the current number of voters, which expression represents the expected number of voters?

   A. $v + 0.73v$
   B. $v + 0.073v$
   C. $1 + 0.73v$
   D. $v + 0.073$

   7.EE.2

TIP of the DAY

Probability is determined by the number of possible outcomes.

WEEK 13 : DAY 5

ASSESSMENT

There are some animals at a wild animal rescue. The animal type and number are shown below. **Use the table below to answer questions 1 – 3.**

Animal	Number
Chimpanzee	16
Bear	7
Bobcat	5
Wolf	7

1. Based on the data, if an animal were randomly picked to be the first one to have its food delivered, what is the probability that a bobcat would be chosen first?

   A. $\frac{1}{5}$ C. $\frac{12}{35}$

   B. $\frac{1}{7}$ D. $\frac{16}{35}$

   7.SP.7

2. Based on the data, if an animal were randomly picked to be the first one to have its food delivered, what is the probability that a bear would be chosen first?

   A. $\frac{1}{5}$ C. $\frac{12}{35}$

   B. $\frac{1}{7}$ D. $\frac{16}{35}$

   7.SP.7

3. Based on the data, if an animal were randomly picked to be the first one to have its food delivered, what is the probability that either a wolf OR a bobcat would be chosen first?

   A. $\frac{1}{5}$ C. $\frac{12}{35}$

   B. $\frac{1}{7}$ D. $\frac{16}{35}$

   7.SP.7

4. There are 100 socks in the laundry hamper. Twenty-four are black, 19 are blue, 12 are red and the rest are white. If Malachi randomly picks a sock from the hamper, what is the probability that he will NOT pick a white sock?

   A. $\frac{9}{20}$

   B. $\frac{11}{20}$

   C. $\frac{3}{25}$

   D. $\frac{6}{25}$

   7.SP.7

DAY 6 Challenge question

There is a 6-sided die. What is the probability that Macie will roll a 3 two times in a row?

7.SP.8

Did you find Week 13 pretty easy? This week you can step it up a notch. We are talking COMPOUND events this week! You can find these probabilities by using charts, diagrams, and simulations you create!

You can find detailed video explanations of each problem in the book by visiting: ArgoPrep.com/ccm7

WEEK 14 : DAY 1

There are 2 fair dice. **Use this pair of dice to answer questions 1 – 2.**

1. How many possible outcomes are there if both dice are thrown at the same time?

   A. 6
   B. 12
   C. 24
   D. 36

   7.SP.8

2. What is the probability that both dice will roll a 2 if they are both thrown at the same time?

   A. $\frac{1}{6}$
   B. $\frac{1}{12}$
   C. $\frac{1}{18}$
   D. $\frac{1}{36}$

   7.SP.8

3. Which scenario is the only one that would fit the probability model shown below?

   | H | T | T | H | H |

   A. There is a 5-sided object that is thrown 5 times.
   B. There are 5 fair coins that are thrown 5 times.
   C. There are 5 different colored cards in a deck.
   D. There are 5 fair coins that are thrown at the same time.

   7.SP.8

4. Which scenario is the only one that would fit the probability model shown below?

   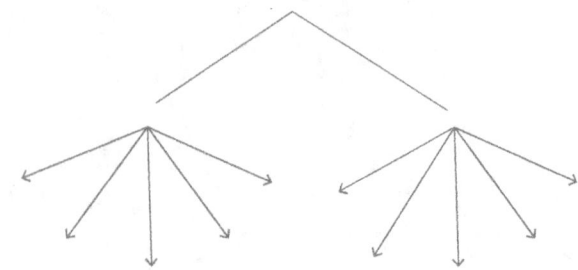

   A. Omar had 2 pairs of pants and 5 shirts he could wear.
   B. Penny had 2 pizzas and 10 desserts from which to choose.
   C. Nathan could choose between a car or 5 bicycles.
   D. Quinn had 1 type of pie filling and 5 types of cookies.

   7.SP.8

5. Nixon makes $8.14 an hour and Mallory makes $12.21 an hour. If Nixon worked 12 hours and Mallory worked 10 hours, how much more money did Mallory make?

   A. $24.42
   B. $42.72
   C. $78.72
   D. $94.52

   7.NS.3

TIP of the DAY

A compound event is one in which there is more than 1 required outcome.

WEEK 14 : DAY 2

1. Which scenario is the only one that would fit the probability model shown below?

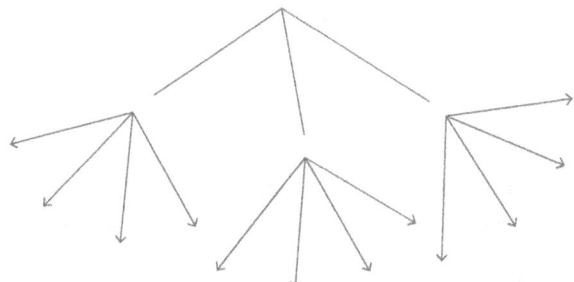

   A. There are 3 fair coins being tossed 4 times.
   B. Olivia has 3 pairs of jeans and 3 pairs of shoes.
   C. Orrin has 12 types of candy to choose from.
   D. Nia can choose 3 types of bread and 4 types of meat.

   7.SP.8

2. What is the probability that Maria can have 2 fair coins that she tosses and get 2 heads on both?

   A. $\frac{1}{2}$
   B. $\frac{1}{4}$
   C. $\frac{1}{8}$
   D. $\frac{1}{16}$

3. There is a penny and a 7-sided cube. What is the probability that Lincoln can roll a tail on the penny AND a 6 on the cube?

   A. $\frac{1}{14}$
   B. $\frac{1}{12}$
   C. $\frac{1}{7}$
   D. $\frac{1}{6}$

   7.SP.8

Ollie has 2 fair dice, each one numbered 1 – 6. **Use this information to answer questions 4 – 5.**

4. What is the probability of rolling the dice and having the 2 dice have a sum of 7?

   A. $\frac{1}{6}$
   B. $\frac{1}{12}$
   C. $\frac{1}{18}$
   D. $\frac{7}{36}$

   7.SP.8

5. What is the probability of rolling the dice and having the 2 dice have a sum of 11?

   A. $\frac{1}{6}$
   B. $\frac{1}{12}$
   C. $\frac{1}{18}$
   D. $\frac{7}{36}$

   7.SP.8

TIP of the DAY

There is a 1 in 2 probability that a fair coin will land on heads when flipped in the air.

WEEK 14 : DAY 3

1. Which scenario is the only one that would fit the probability model shown below?

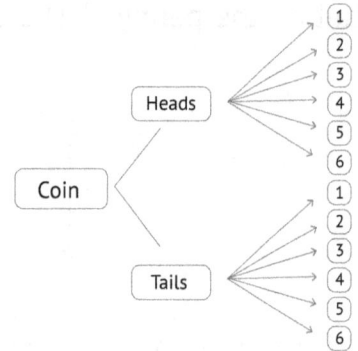

   A. Prim rolls a 6-sided cube then flips a fair coin.
   B. Opal flips a fair coin then rolls a fair die.
   C. Quenton rolls a fair coin twice then rolls a fair die.
   D. Naomi flips a fair coin then rolls a fair die six times.

   7.SP.8

There are 4 cards (each card is a different color), 1 six-sided die, and 2 coins. **Use this information to answer questions 2 – 5.**

2. What is the probability that Peri can draw a green card, get a head on both coins and roll a 3?

   A. $\frac{1}{32}$
   B. $\frac{1}{48}$
   C. $\frac{1}{72}$
   D. $\frac{1}{96}$

   7.SP.8

3. What is the probability that Mille can get a head on 1 coin and roll a 5 on the die?

   A. $\frac{1}{4}$ B. $\frac{1}{6}$ C. $\frac{1}{12}$ D. $\frac{1}{24}$

   7.SP.8

4. What is the probability that Ric can get a tail on both coins and pick a blue card?

   A. $\frac{1}{4}$ B. $\frac{1}{8}$ C. $\frac{1}{16}$ D. $\frac{1}{32}$

   7.SP.8

5. What is the probability that Nolan can roll a 4 on the die and pick a red card?

   A. $\frac{1}{4}$ B. $\frac{1}{6}$ C. $\frac{1}{12}$ D. $\frac{1}{24}$

   7.SP.8

6. The probability that Oxana will score a basket is $\frac{1}{4}$. The probability that Harold will score a basket is $\frac{1}{3}$. What is the probability that both Oxana and Harold will score?

   A. $\frac{1}{7}$ B. $\frac{1}{8}$ C. $\frac{1}{12}$ D. $\frac{1}{14}$

   7.SP.8

TIP of the DAY

Remember when there are compound events, you multiply the probabilities of each event to find the probability of the compound events.

WEEK 14 : DAY 4

1. Using only one 8-sided cube, what is the probability that Percy can roll a 5 OR a 7 on three straight rolls?

   A. $\dfrac{1}{16}$
   B. $\dfrac{1}{32}$
   C. $\dfrac{1}{64}$
   D. $\dfrac{1}{256}$

   7.SP.8

2. Which fraction shows the probability that Patti will flip a heads, a tail and then heads again on a fair coin?

   A. $\dfrac{1}{2}$
   B. $\dfrac{1}{4}$
   C. $\dfrac{1}{6}$
   D. $\dfrac{1}{8}$

   7.SP.8

3. If the probability of Rhoda drawing a purple marble from a bag is $\dfrac{1}{9}$ and she draws 1 marble at a time and replaces it, how many times would you expect Rhoda to get a purple marble if she tries 360 times?

   A. 18
   B. 36
   C. 40
   D. 81

   7.SP.6

4. What is the constant of proportionality for the table shown below?

x	y
2	4
4	8
5	10

   A. $\dfrac{1}{2}$
   B. $\dfrac{1}{4}$
   C. 2
   D. 4

   7.RP.2

5. A pound of turkey costs $1.89. What equation is used to find C, the total cost for t pounds of turkey?

   A. $C = 1.89t$
   B. $C = 1.89 + t$
   C. $C + 1.89 = t$
   D. $t = 1.89c$

   7.RP.2

TIP of the DAY

The probability of flipping a tail on a fair coin is $\dfrac{1}{2}$. The probability of getting a tail on a fair coin two times in a row is $\dfrac{1}{4}$ because $\dfrac{1}{2} \times \dfrac{1}{2} = \dfrac{1}{4}$.

WEEK 14 : DAY 5

ASSESSMENT

Below is a list of the items that students have available to them. **Use this information to answer questions 1 – 3.**

Quantity	Item
2	Deck of 5 cards, each with a different color
3	6-sided cube lettered A – F
5	Fair coin (heads/tails)

1. What is the probability that Ophelia can roll tails on all 5 coins?

   A. $\dfrac{1}{8}$ C. $\dfrac{1}{24}$

   B. $\dfrac{1}{16}$ D. $\dfrac{1}{32}$

   7.SP.8

2. What is the probability that Robert can get a tail using 1 coin and pick a yellow card from 1 deck and roll an E on 1 cube?

   A. $\dfrac{1}{10}$ C. $\dfrac{1}{60}$

   B. $\dfrac{1}{30}$ D. $\dfrac{1}{90}$

   7.SP.8

3. What is the probability that Martin can use 2 decks of cards and 3 cubes to pick 2 yellow cards and roll a D on 3 cubes?

   A. $\dfrac{1}{4}$ C. $\dfrac{1}{540}$

   B. $\dfrac{1}{54}$ D. $\dfrac{1}{5400}$

   7.SP.8

4. Using a fair 6-sided die, numbered 1- 6, what is the probability that a person can roll a 4 three times in a row?

   A. $\dfrac{1}{64}$ C. $\dfrac{1}{216}$

   B. $\dfrac{1}{108}$ D. $\dfrac{1}{532}$

   7.SP.8

5. Each hour Hayden is able to run 9 kilometers. If he has already run 5 kilometers, what will his total distance be after 7 hours?

   A. 44 kilometers
   B. 45 kilometers
   C. 52 kilometers
   D. 68 kilometers

   7.SP.8

DAY 6
Challenge question

Using the items from questions 1 – 5, what is the probability that a person could get all heads on all coins, a 2 on all cubes and pick all blue cards in one try?

7.SP.8

Have you ever wondered about being an architect or a construction worker? In Week 15 we explore scale models and compare them to their actual rooms/buildings/heights. This week you'll get practice working with blueprints and using scale models.

You can find detailed video explanations of each problem in the book by visiting:
ArgoPrep.com/ccm7

WEEK 15 : DAY 1

1. The scale model of a boat is 1 cm to 4.5 meters. If the real boat is 63 meters, what is the length, in cm, of the model boat?

   A. 9 cm   C. 14 cm
   B. 12 cm D. 18 cm

2. The diagram below shows the dimensions of Carmen's dining room. If a scale model were built so that 5 centimeters on the model represented 1 foot of the actual room, what would be the length, in centimeters, of the model?

   A. 2 centimeters
   B. 15 centimeters
   C. 25 centimeters
   D. 50 centimeters

3. What is the decimal equivalent of $\frac{7}{5}$?

   A. 1.2   C. 5.7
   B. 1.4   D. 7.5

4. The blueprint for a barn has a scale where 1.5 inches on the blueprint represents 4 feet on the actual barn. If the barn on the blueprint has a height of 12 inches, what is the height of the actual barn?

   A. 8 feet   C. 32 feet
   B. 16 feet   D. 48 feet

5. The scale model of a statue is 1 inch to 11.2 feet. If the model is 5.8 inches, what is the length, in feet, of the actual statue?

   A. 17.00 feet   C. 50.12 feet
   B. 34.86 feet   D. 64.96 feet

6. The postmaster had $2\frac{1}{5}$ inches of mail on his desk when he left for vacation. While he was gone for 6 days, his mail pile grew by 1.3 inches each day. How tall would the pile of mail be when the postmaster returned?

   A. $9\frac{1}{2}$ inches   C. $10\frac{3}{10}$ inches
   B. 10 inches   D. 21 inches

TIP of the DAY: A scale model means that every dimension in the model is the same proportion to the real object's corresponding dimension.

WEEK 15 : DAY 2

1. The diagram below shows a scale model of Roscoe's garage. If the scale model is built so that 1 inch on the model represents 2.5 feet on the actual garage, what would be the width, in feet, of the garage?

Length: 15 inches
Width: 10.5 inches

A. 20.5 feet
B. 26.25 feet
C. 37.5 feet
D. 42.25 feet

7.G.1

2. The scale model of a train is 1.5 inches to 2 yards. If the real train has an engine car that is 20 yards, what is the length, in inches, of the model engine car?

A. 7.5 inches
B. 15 inches
C. 30 inches
D. 37.5 inches

7.G.1

3. The blueprint of a door has a key where 2 inches = 1.5 feet. If the door on the blueprint is 9 inches tall, what is the height, in feet, of the actual door?

A. 6 feet
B. 6.25 feet
C. 6.5 feet
D. 6.75 feet

7.G.1

4. If there is a die that has 12 sides that are numbered 1 – 12, what is the probability that Shana will roll either a 3 or a 9?

A. $\frac{1}{3}$ C. $\frac{1}{6}$

B. $\frac{1}{4}$ D. $\frac{1}{12}$

7.SP.7

5. The blueprint of a desk is 1 inch to 2.3 feet. If the actual desk is 6.9 feet long, what is the length, in inches, on the blueprint?

A. 3.0 inches
B. 4.6 inches
C. 5.4 inches
D. 6.9 inches

7.G.1

TIP of the DAY

A scale model is often used to help us understand something that is either very large or very small.

97

WEEK 15 : DAY 3

There is a storage building that has several sides and it has a scale model where 1 inch on the model represents 3.5 yards of the actual building. **Use this information to answer questions 1 – 3.**

1. If a side on the scale model is 12 inches, what is the approximate length of the corresponding side of the actual storage building?

   A. 3 yards
   B. 40 yards
   C. 42 yards
   D. 54.2 yards
   7.G.1

2. If a side on the actual storage building is 66 <u>feet</u>, what is the approximate length of the corresponding side of the scale model?

   A. 6.3 inches
   B. 12.6 inches
   C. 15.3 inches
   D. 18.6 inches
   7.G.1

3. If a side on the scale model is 4.5 inches, what is the approximate length of the corresponding side of the actual storage building?

   A. 0.78 yards
   B. 1.29 yards
   C. 15.75 yards
   D. 47.25 yards
   7.G.1

The diagram below shows a scale model of a cell membrane. The scale model is designed so that 1 inch on the model represents 0.5 millimeters on the actual cell membrane. **Use this model to answer questions 4 – 5.**

Length: 9 inches
Width: 8 inches

4. What is the width, in millimeters, of the membrane?

   A. 4.0 mm
   B. 4.5 mm
   C. 8 mm
   D. 8.5 mm
   7.G.1

5. What is the length, in millimeters, of the membrane?

   A. 4.0 mm
   B. 4.5 mm
   C. 8 mm
   D. 8.5 mm
   7.G.1

6. What is the product of $\left(-\dfrac{3}{4}\right) \times \left(-\dfrac{12}{7}\right)$?

   A. $1\dfrac{5}{16}$
   B. $-1\dfrac{5}{16}$
   C. $-1\dfrac{2}{7}$
   D. $1\dfrac{2}{7}$
   7.NS.2

TIP of the DAY

You are doing a great job – keep up the hard work! By completing this workbook, you will have learned a LOT that should help you on your tests!

WEEK 15 : DAY 4

The diagram below shows a scale model of the floor of a doghouse. The scale model is designed so that 1 cm on the model represents 0.6 feet on the actual doghouse. **Use this model to answer questions 1 – 2.**

1. What is the width, in feet, of the doghouse?

   A. 2.4 feet
   B. 4.5 feet
   C. 6.7 feet
   D. 12.5 feet

   7.G.1

2. What is the length, in feet, of the doghouse?

   A. 2.4 feet
   B. 4.5 feet
   C. 6.7 feet
   D. 12.5 feet

   7.G.1

3. The scale model of a car is 1 mm to 1.7 meters. If the real car is 6.8 meters, what is the length, in mm, of the model car?

   A. 2 mm   C. 6 mm
   B. 4 mm   D. 8 mm

   7.G.1

4. There is a deck of 5 cards that are labeled A – E. What is the probability that a player will draw a B card three times in a row?

   A. $\frac{1}{5}$ C. $\frac{1}{125}$
   B. $\frac{1}{25}$ D. $\frac{1}{625}$

   7.SP.8

5. The scale model of a table is 1 cm to 1.2 feet. If the real table is 6 feet, what is the length, in cm, of the model table?

   A. 2.2 cm   C. 7.2 cm
   B. 5.0 cm   D. 9.0 cm

   7.G.1

6. Which property is shown below?

   $(12a + a) + 5a = 12a + (a + 5a)$

   A. Associative Property
   B. Commutative Property
   C. Distributive Property
   D. Inverse Property

   7.EE.1

TIP of the DAY

A scale model is not always smaller than the actual item. In science a model can be used to show something that is very small like a cell or DNA.

99

WEEK 15 : DAY 5

ASSESSMENT

There is a building that has 6 sides and it has a scale model where 3 cm on the model represents 5 feet of the actual building. **Use this information to answer questions 1 – 3.**

1. If a side on the scale model is 10.5 cm, what is the length of the corresponding side of the actual building?

   A. 15.0 feet
   B. 17.5 feet
   C. 37.0 feet
   D. 52.5 feet

   7.G.1

2. If a side on the actual building is 22 feet, what is the approximate length of the corresponding side of the scale model?

   A. 13.2 cm
   B. 24.5 cm
   C. 33.0 cm
   D. 36.7 cm

   7.G.1

3. If a side on the scale model is 20 cm, what is the approximate length of the corresponding side of the actual building?

   A. 12.0 feet
   B. 24.3 feet
   C. 30.0 feet
   D. 33.3 feet

   7.G.1

4. Below are some transactions that Steffy made with her bank account.

Deposits	Withdrawals
619.75	134.62
200	48.09

   If Steffy's account had $412.89 before any deposits or withdrawals, what was her final balance?

   A. − $224.15
   B. $1002.46
   C. $1049.93
   D. $1232.64

   7.NS.1

5. The blueprint of a closet has a scale that is 2.5 cm to 1.5 feet. If the real closet is 8 feet tall, what is the approximate height, in inches, on the blueprint?

   A. 4.8 cm
   B. 13.3 cm
   C. 26.6 cm
   D. 30.0 cm

   7.G.1

6. The scale model of a chair is 1 inch (model) to 1.5 feet (actual). If the actual chair is 7 feet, what is the approximate length, in inches, of the model chair?

   A. 2.8 inches
   B. 4.7 inches
   C. 8.5 inches
   D. 10.5 inches

   7.G.1

DAY 6 Challenge question

There is a building that has a scale model where 2 cm on the model represents 3 meters of the actual building. If the length and the width of the model are 5 cm and 7 cm, what are the dimensions of the actual building?

7.G.1

WEEK 16

VIDEO EXPLANATIONS
ARGOPREP.COM

Week 16 is all about triangles! You will have a chance to measure and determine the angle measures of triangles. You will also be able to identify specific types of triangles as well as other geometric shapes.

You can find detailed video explanations of each problem in the book by visiting: ArgoPrep.com/ccm7

WEEK 16 : DAY 1

There are 4 shapes shown below. **Use this information to answer questions 1 – 3.**

Shape	Angle 1	Angle 2	Angle 3	Side 1	Side 2	Side 3
A	30°	60°	90°	6.1 in	10.6 in	12.2 in
B	97°	48°	35°	34.4 cm	24.3 cm	9.9 cm
C	24°	99°	58°	12.7 mm	30.8 mm	26.2 mm
D	68°	77°	35°	25.3 ft	26.6 ft	15.7 ft

1. Which shape is a right triangle?

   A. A
   B. B
   C. B
   D. C

   7.G.2

2. Which shape has angle measures that indicate it can NOT be a triangle?

   A. A
   B. B
   C. C
   D. D

   7.G.2

3. Which shape has side lengths that indicate it can NOT be a triangle?

   A. A
   B. B
   C. C
   D. D

   7.G.2

4. There is a triangle that has 2 angles that measure 12° and 105°. What is the measure of the third angle?

   A. 63°
   B. 73°
   C. 153°
   D. 243°

   7.G.2

5. There is a triangle that has 2 angles that measure 13° and 127°. What is the measure of the third angle?

   A. 40°
   B. 60°
   C. 120°
   D. 180°

   7.G.2

TIP of the DAY

The 3 angles in a triangle should equal 180° when their angle measures are added together.

WEEK 16 : DAY 2

1. There is a triangle that has 2 sides that measure 16.8 inches and 8.2 inches. Which of the measurements below can **NOT** be the 3rd side?

   A. 7.8 inches
   B. 8.9 inches
   C. 9.1 inches
   D. 9.7 inches

   7.G.2

2. There is a triangle that has 2 angles that measure 67.1° and 8.9°. What is the measure of the third angle?

   A. 84°
   B. 94°
   C. 104°
   D. 194°

   7.G.2

3. There is a triangle that has 2 angles that measure 102° and 35°. What is the measure of the third angle?

   A. 33°
   B. 43°
   C. 87°
   D. 137°

   7.G.2

4. You are to solve the equation:

   $$13y = -8.2$$

   What step should you take first?

   A. Add 8.2
   B. Subtract 8.2
   C. Multiply by 13
   D. Divide by 13

   7.EE.4

5. There is a triangle that has 2 angles that measure 14.7° and 98.3°. What is the measure of the third angle?

   A. 43.6°
   B. 57.0°
   C. 67.0°
   D. 77.0°

   7.G.2

6. Which expression represents a factorization of $65m - 39mn$?

   A. $13(5m - 3n)$
   B. $13m(5m - 3n)$
   C. $13m(3n - 5)$
   D. $13m(5 - 3n)$

   7.EE.1

An acute triangle has 3 angles that are all less than 90 degrees.

WEEK 16 : DAY 3

There are 4 shapes shown below. **Use this information to answer questions 1 – 3.**

Shape	Angle 1	Angle 2	Angle 3	Side 1	Side 2	Side 3
A	34°	112°	34°	14.2 yds	23.5 yds	14.2 yds
B	25°	29°	126°	10.5 cm	12 cm	20.1 cm
C	54°	86°	38°	14.3 m	17.6 m	11.4 m
D	53°	56°	71°	12.6 in	13.2 in	25.9 in

1. Which shape has angle measures that indicate it can NOT be a triangle?

   A. A
   B. B
   C. C
   D. D

   7.G.2

2. Which shape has side lengths that indicate it can NOT be a triangle?

   A. A
   B. B
   C. C
   D. D

   7.G.2

3. Which shape is an isosceles triangle?

   A. A
   B. B
   C. C
   D. D

   7.G.2

4. The city government wants to know which sport is the most popular at the city park. Which population would be the best group to ask?

   A. Every 5th person at the city park
   B. Every 10th taxpayer
   C. All of the coaches that play at the city park
   D. Every 10th city park baseball player

   7.SP.1

5. There is a triangle that has 2 angles that measure 108° and 17°. What is the measure of the third angle?

   A. 35°
   B. 40°
   C. 45°
   D. 55°

   7.G.2

TIP of the DAY

Remember that when 2 sides of a triangle are added together, their sum must be greater than the length of the third side.

WEEK 16 : DAY 4

1. There is a triangle that has 2 angles that measure 18.4° and 72.9°. What is the measure of the third angle?

   A. 44.5°
   B. 88.7°
   C. 91.3°
   D. 137.0°

   7.G.2

2. There is a triangle that has 2 sides that measure 4.8 cm and 3.9 cm. Which of the measurements below can the 3rd side NOT be?

   A. 2.9 cm
   B. 4.5 cm
   C. 6.0 cm
   D. 8.8 cm

   7.G.2

3. The probability of Xander drawing a gray stone from a bag is $\frac{2}{7}$. He draws 1 stone at a time and replaces it. How many times would you expect Xander to get a gray stone if he tries 784 times?

   A. 112   C. 224
   B. 168   D. 296

   7.SP.6

4. There is a right triangle that has a side that is 45 degrees. How many degrees is the third angle

   A. 45°
   B. 90°
   C. 135°
   D. 225°

   7.G.2

5. The sofa was priced at $1298. The store discounted it by 20% for 1 week. The next week they increased the price by 5%. What is the price now?

   A. $1038.40
   B. $1090.32
   C. $1103.30
   D. $1633.50

   7.RP.3

6. Using only one 9-sided cube, what is the probability that Ursula will roll a 3, 4 OR 7 on three straight rolls?

   A. $\frac{1}{3}$ C. $\frac{1}{27}$
   B. $\frac{1}{9}$ D. $\frac{1}{81}$

   7.SP.8

TIP of the DAY

Before taking tomorrow's assessment, please be sure to have any tools you may need – a ruler, protractor, calculator and plenty of pencils and paper.

105

WEEK 16 : DAY 5

ASSESSMENT

There are 4 shapes shown below. **Use this information to answer questions 1 – 3.**

Shape	Angle 1	Angle 2	Angle 3	Side 1	Side 2	Side 3
A	68°	53°	59°	16.4 m	14.1 m	15.2 m
B	22°	136°	24°	14.2 in	26.3 in	14.2 in
C	54°	19°	107°	19.1 cm	7.7 cm	22.6 cm
D	92°	37°	51°	13.8 ft	8.3 ft	1.7 ft

1. Which shape has side lengths that indicate it can NOT be a triangle?

   A. A   C. C
   B. B   D. D

   7.G.2

2. Which shape is an acute triangle?

   A. A   C. C
   B. B   D. D

   7.G.2

3. Which shape has angle measures that indicate it can NOT be a triangle?

   A. A
   B. B
   C. C
   D. D

   7.G.2

4. There is a triangle that has 2 angles that measure 92.3° and 29°. What is the measure of the third angle?

   A. 48.3°
   B. 58.7°
   C. 68.3°
   D. 148.7°

   7.G.2

5. Yulia is spinning a spinner. The probability that the spinner will land on 4 on her next turn is $\frac{1}{3}$. Which statement describes the probability that Yulia's next spin will be a 4?

   A. likely
   B. certain
   C. unlikely
   D. impossible

   7.SP.5

DAY 6
Challenge question

There is a right triangle that has an angle that is 17 degrees. How many degrees is the 3rd side of the triangle?

7.G.2

106

WEEK 17

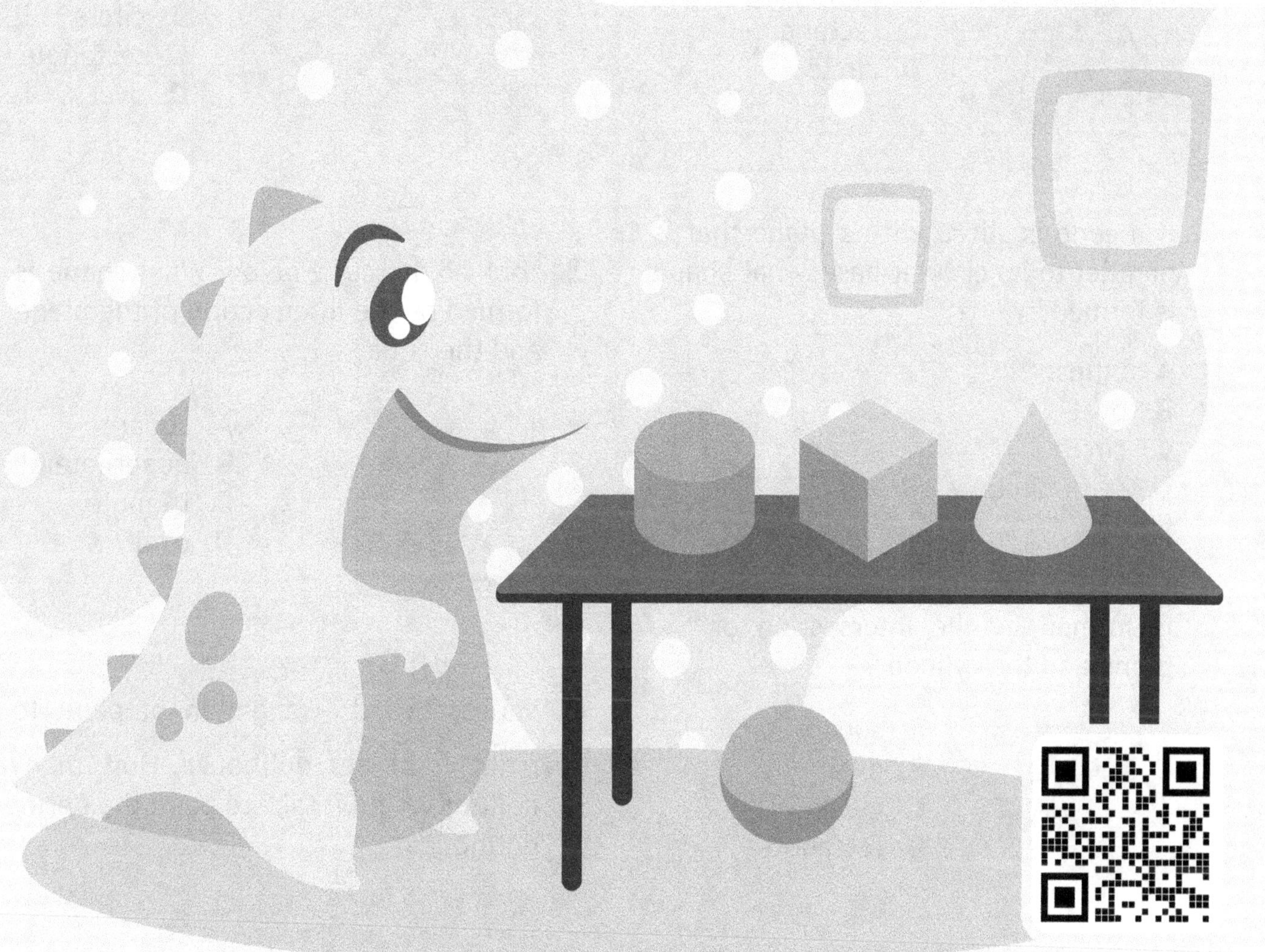

Have you ever cut a piece of wood and wondered about the shape that is made? This week you will have lots of practice "cutting" open shapes and "seeing" how the shapes changed based simply on the way the shape is cut. Perpendicular and parallel cuts form different shapes from cuts that are not perpendicular or parallel.

WEEK 17 : DAY 1

1. Look at the pyramid below. What shape is formed by the intersection of the plane and the pyramid?

   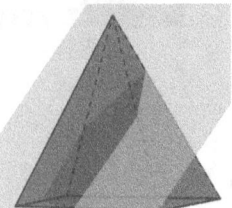

   A. pentagon
   B. parallelogram
   C. rectangle
   D. circle

   7.G.3

2. If a cone is sliced with a plane that is parallel to its circular base, what shape is formed?

   A. ellipse
   B. oval
   C. circle
   D. semi-circle

   7.G.3

3. Look at the cylinder below. What shape is formed by the intersection of the plane and the cylinder?

   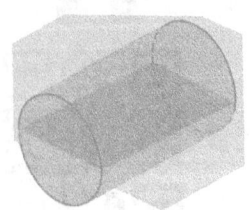

   A. square
   B. oval
   C. circle
   D. rectangle

   7.G.3

4. Look at the cone below. There is an intersecting plane that is parallel to the base of the cone. What shape is formed by the intersection of the plane and the cone?

   A. triangle
   B. circle
   C. rectangle
   D. oval

   7.G.3

5. Look at the cube below. What shape is formed by the intersection of the plane and the cube?

   A. square
   B. quadrilateral
   C. triangle
   D. oval

   7.G.3

6. Vanessa used $\frac{1}{2}$ a gallon of paint to paint $\frac{3}{4}$ of her dollhouse. How many gallons would it take to paint the entire dollhouse?

   A. $\frac{1}{6}$ B. $\frac{5}{6}$ C. $\frac{1}{3}$ D. $\frac{2}{3}$

   7.RP.1

TIP of the DAY

When three-dimensional shapes are sliced, they can produce different shapes dependent on how the shape is sliced.

WEEK 17 : DAY 2

1. If a pyramid is sliced with a plane that is parallel to its square base, what shape is formed?

   A. square
   B. rectangle
   C. pentagon
   D. triangle

   7.G.3

2. Look at the cone below. What shape is formed by the intersection of the plane and the cone?

   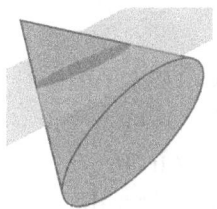

   A. rectangle
   B. triangle
   C. oval
   D. circle

   7.G.3

3. Look at the sphere below. What shape is formed by the intersection of the plane and the sphere?

   A. oval
   B. square
   C. trapezoid
   D. circle

   7.G.3

4. If a cone is sliced with a plane that is perpendicular to its circular base and goes through its endpoint, what shape is formed?

   A. triangle
   B. cone
   C. circle
   D. trapezoid

   7.G.3

5. Look at the cylinder below. What shape is formed by the intersection of the plane and the cylinder?

   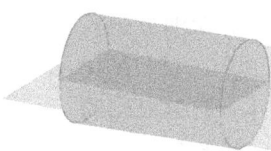

   A. oval
   B. rectangle
   C. square
   D. circle

   7.G.3

6. The model of a car has a scale where 3 inches = 1.5 feet. If the model is 9 inches long, what is the length, in feet, of the actual car?

   A. 3 feet
   B. 3.5 feet
   C. 4.5 feet
   D. 5.5 feet

   7.G.1

TIP of the DAY

No matter how a plane slices a sphere, if the plane goes completely through the sphere, the intersection will form a circle.

WEEK 17 : DAY 3

1. If a horizontal slice of the cone below is removed, what two-dimensional shape will the slice be?

   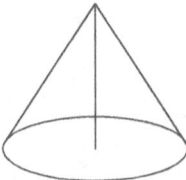

   A. oval
   B. triangle
   C. ellipse
   D. circle

   7.G.3

2. Below is a rectangular prism that has a square base. If it were sliced by a horizontal plane, what shape would be created?

   A. square
   B. rectangle
   C. trapezoid
   D. kite

   7.G.3

3. Look at the cube below. What shape is formed by the intersection of the plane and the cube?

   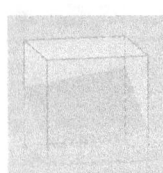

   A. pentagon
   B. hexagon
   C. quadrilateral
   D. square

   7.G.3

4. Below is a picture of a sphere being sliced by a plane. What two-dimensional shape does this slice create?

   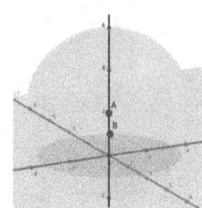

   A. oval
   B. triangle
   C. ellipse
   D. circle

   7.G.3

5. Look at the cylinder below. What shape is formed by the intersection of the plane and the cylinder?

   A. rectangle
   B. oval
   C. circle
   D. triangle

   7.G.3

6. Vicky started with $110. She paid back $32 to her brother. Then her sister borrowed $17. Which expression could be used to find how much money Vicky now has?

   A. 110 + 32 − 17 = 125
   B. 110 − 32 + 17 = 95
   C. 110 + 32 + 17 = 159
   D. 110 − 32 − 17 = 61

   7.NS.1

TIP of the DAY

When finding 2-dimensional shapes made from 3-dimensional shapes that are "cut" with a plane, be sure to check and see if the plane is parallel or perpendicular.

WEEK 17 : DAY 4

1. Below is a picture of a cylinder being sliced by a horizontal plane. What two-dimensional shape does this slice create?

   A. circle
   B. triangle
   C. ellipse
   D. oval

   7.G.3

2. If a pyramid is sliced with a plane that is perpendicular to its square base and goes through the vertex, what shape is formed?

   A. square
   B. rectangle
   C. pentagon
   D. triangle

   7.G.3

3. There is a sphere that is sliced by a vertical plane. What shape is created by this slicing?

   A. oval
   B. circle
   C. rectangle
   D. point

   7.G.3

4. The cone below is being sliced by a horizontal plane. What two-dimensional shape is created at the intersection of the cone and the plane?

   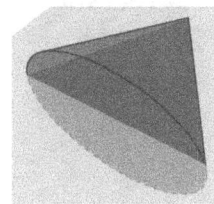

   A. rectangle
   B. triangle
   C. circle
   D. ellipse

   7.G.3

5. Look at the cube below. What shape is formed by the intersection of the plane and the cube?

   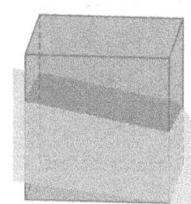

   A. square
   B. pentagon
   C. triangle
   D. rectangle

   7.G.3

6. The blueprint for a grocery store has a scale where 2 inches on the blueprint represents 10 feet on the actual store. If the store on the blueprint has a length of 13 inches, what is the length of the actual store?

   A. 6.5 feet
   B. 13 feet
   C. 65 feet
   D. 130 feet

   7.G.1

TIP of the DAY

When finding 2-dimensional shapes made from 3-dimensional shapes that are "cut" with a plane, be sure to check the number of sides on the base of the 3-dimensional shape.

WEEK 17 : DAY 5

ASSESSMENT

1. What two-dimensional shape is created by the intersection of the cylinder and the horizontal plane shown below?

   A. rectangle
   B. circle
   C. square
   D. oval

   7.G.3

2. Look at the sphere below. What shape is formed by the intersection of the plane and the sphere?

   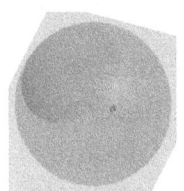

   A. circle
   B. square
   C. trapezoid
   D. oval

   7.G.3

3. The pyramid below has a square base. What shape is formed by the intersection of the plane and the pyramid? Note: the plane is NOT horizontal.

   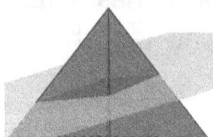

   A. rectangle
   B. rhombus
   C. quadrilateral
   D. parallelogram

   7.G.3

4. There is a cube that is sliced by a vertical plane. What shape does this slicing create?

   A. square
   B. rectangle
   C. trapezoid
   D. kite

   7.G.3

5. Look at the cube below. What shape is formed by the intersection of the plane and the cube?

   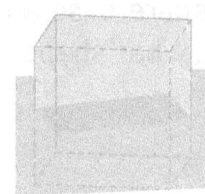

   A. square
   B. quadrilateral
   C. pentagon
   D. triangle

   7.G.3

6. What two-dimensional shape is created by the intersection of the pyramid and the horizontal plane shown below?

   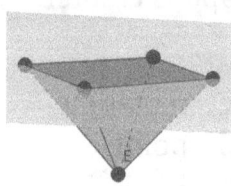

   A. trapezoid
   B. rectangle
   C. triangle
   D. pentagon

   7.G.3

DAY 6
Challenge question

There is a rectangular prism that has 2 bases that both have 10 sides. If a plane parallel to the bases "cuts" the prism, what is the shape that is created?

7.G.3

WEEK 18

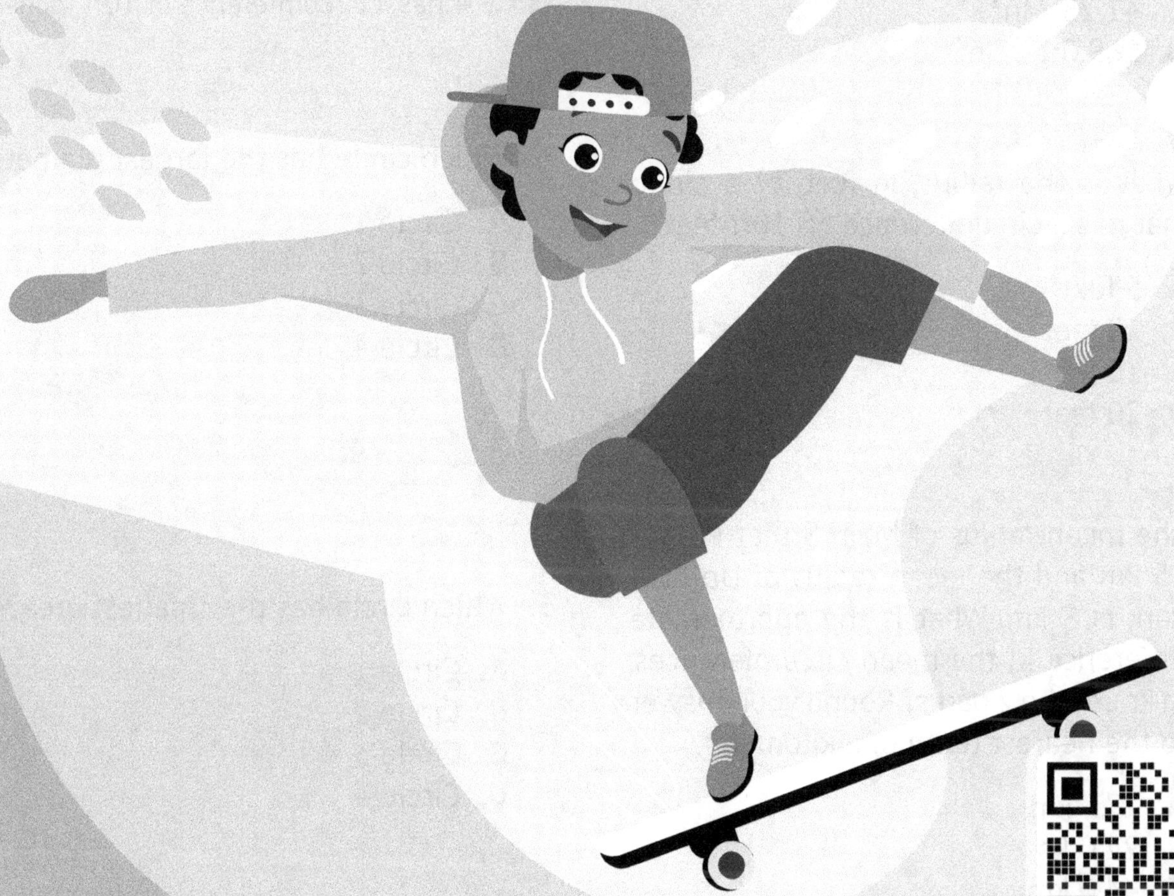

Circles, circles, everywhere! In Week 18 you will be able to investigate the connection between a circle's area and its circumference. To extend your learning, you may be given the area and asked to find the circumference, or vice versa.

You can find detailed video explanations of each problem in the book by visiting: ArgoPrep.com/ccm7

WEEK 18 : DAY 1

1. The circumference of a circle is 13π inches. What is the area, in square inches, of the circle? Express your answer in terms of π.

   A. 6.5π in²
   B. 26.0π in²
   C. 42.25π in²
   D. 169.0π in in²

   7.G.4

2. What is the radius, in feet, of a circle that has a circumference of 10π feet?

   A. 5 feet
   B. 10 feet
   C. 15 feet
   D. 20 feet

   7.G.4

3. The mean radius of Main Street Park is 15 km and the mean radius of Uptown Park is 8 km. What is the approximate difference in the mean circumferences, in km, of the 2 parks? Round your answer to the nearest tenth of a kilometer.

   A. 17.1 km
   B. 22.0 km
   C. 44.0 km
   D. 87.9 km

   7.G.4

There is information about 4 circles shown below. **Use the given information to answer questions 4 – 5.**

Circle **1** has a radius of 8 inches.
Circle **2** has a diameter of 24 inches.
Circle **3** has an area of 100π inches².
Circle **4** has a circumference of 10π inches.

4. Which circle has the largest diameter?

   A. Circle 1
   B. Circle 2
   C. Circle 3
   D. Circle 4

   7.G.4

5. Which circle has the smallest area?

   A. Circle 1
   B. Circle 2
   C. Circle 3
   D. Circle 4

   7.G.4

TIP of the DAY

The circumference of a circle is pi times the diameter of the circle.

WEEK 18 : DAY 2

1. The circumference of a circle is 7π inches. What is the area, in square inches, of the circle? Express your answer in terms of π.

   A. 7π in²
   B. 12.25π in²
   C. 14π in²
   D. 49π in²

   7.G.4

2. The mean radius of the interstate bypass is 25 miles and the mean radius of the actual interstate is 16 miles. What is the approximate difference in the mean circumferences, in miles, of the 2 expressways? Round your answer to the nearest tenth of a mile.

   A. 9.0 miles
   B. 28.3 miles
   C. 32.0 miles
   D. 56.5 miles

   7.G.4

3. What is the radius, in cm, of a circle that has an area of 36π cm²?

   A. 3 cm
   B. 4 cm
   C. 6 cm
   D. 9 cm

   7.G.4

4. There is a triangle that has 2 angles that measure 113° and 17°. What is the measure of the third angle?

   A. 50°
   B. 70°
   C. 130°
   D. 180°

   7.G.2

5. The mean radius of the chocolate chip cookie is 12 centimeters and the mean radius of the oatmeal cookie is 9 centimeters. What is the approximate difference in the mean circumferences, in centimeters, of the 2 cookies?

   A. 3.14 cm
   B. 9.42 cm
   C. 18.84 cm
   D. 37.68 cm

   7.G.4

6. Look at the cone below. What shape is formed by the intersection of the plane and the cone? (The plane is not parallel or perpendicular to the base of the cone.)

   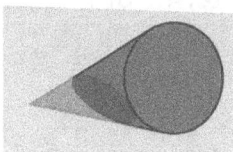

   A. triangle
   B. oval
   C. rectangle
   D. circle

   7.G.3

TIP of the DAY

The circumference of a circle is two times the radius times pi.

115

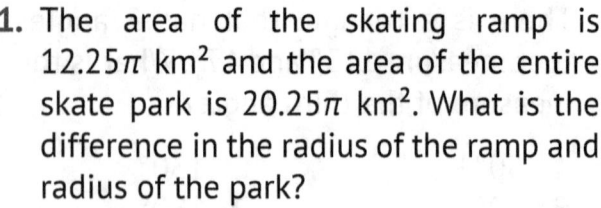

WEEK 18 : DAY 3

1. The area of the skating ramp is 12.25π km² and the area of the entire skate park is 20.25π km². What is the difference in the radius of the ramp and radius of the park?

   A. 1 km
   B. 2 km
   C. 3.5 km
   D. 4.5 km

   7.G.4

2. What is the area, in cm, of a circle that has a diameter of 13 cm? Round your answer to the nearest hundredth of a square cm.

   A. 40.8 cm²
   B. 81.6 cm²
   C. 132.7 cm²
   D. 530.7 cm²

   7.G.4

3. The diameter of a circle is 12 mm. What is the area, in square mm, of the circle? Express your answer in terms of π.

   A. 6π mm²
   B. 18π mm²
   C. 24π mm²
   D. 36π mm²

   7.G.4

There is information about 4 circles shown below. **Use the given information to answer questions 4 – 5.**

Circle 1 has a radius of 10 cm.
Circle 2 has a diameter of 6 cm.
Circle 3 has an area of π cm².
Circle 4 has a circumference of 14π cm.

4. Which circle has the largest area?

   A. Circle 1
   B. Circle 2
   C. Circle 3
   D. Circle 4

   7.G.4

5. Put the circles in order from the one that has the smallest area to the one that has the largest area.

   A. 3241
   B. 1243
   C. 3412
   D. 4321

   7.G.4

TIP of the DAY

To find the area of a circle, square the radius and then multiply by π.

WEEK 18 : DAY 4

There are 4 circles shown below. **Use π ≈ 3.14 and the diagram to answer questions 1 – 4.** Answer choices may have been rounded.

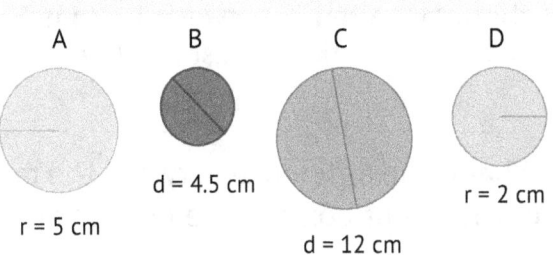

1. What is the area of Circle A?

    A. 15.7 cm²
    B. 78.5 cm²
    C. 196.25 cm²
    D. 246.49 cm²

    7.G.4

2. What is the area of Circle B?

    A. 15.90 cm²
    B. 28.26 cm²
    C. 42.39 cm²
    D. 63.59 cm²

    7.G.4

3. What is the circumference of Circle C?

    A. 9.42 cm
    B. 18.84 cm
    C. 37.68 cm
    D. 113.04 cm

    7.G.4

4. What is the circumference of Circle D?

    A. 3.14 cm
    B. 6.28 cm
    C. 9.42 cm
    D. 12.56 cm

    7.G.4

5. Monday morning it was −5.7°F. If the temperature dropped 1.8°F in the afternoon, what was the temperature in the afternoon?

    A. 3.9°F
    B. 7.5°F
    C. −7.5°F
    D. −3.9°F

    7.NS.1

TIP of the DAY

To prepare for tomorrow's assessment, you can draw and/or measure several different circles and see if you can find the connection between each circle's radius, diameter, circumference and/or area.

WEEK 18 : DAY 5

ASSESSMENT

There is information about 4 circles shown below. **Use the given information to answer questions 1 – 2.**

Circle A has a radius of 7.5 yards.
Circle B has a diameter of 5 yards.
Circle C has a circumference of 12π yards.
Circle D has an area of 16π yards².

1. Which 2 circles have areas that differ by exactly 50π?

   A. Circles A and B
   B. Circles C and D
   C. Circles A and C
   D. Circles B and D

   7.G.4

2. Put the circles in order from the one that has the smallest area to the one that has the largest area.

   A. ADBC
   B. BDCA
   C. CBAD
   D. DCAB

   7.G.4

The area of a circular donut box is 9π cm². The donut hole in the donut has an area that is 0.25π cm².
Use this information to answer questions 3 – 5.
Round answers to the nearest hundredth.

3. What is the difference between the radii of the donut box and the donut hole?

   A. 0.5 cm
   B. 1.5 cm
   C. 2.0 cm
   D. 2.5 cm

   7.G.4

4. What is the area of the donut itself?

   A. 8.25π cm²
   B. 8.5π cm²
   C. 8.75π cm²
   D. 9.25π cm²

   7.G.4

5. What is the difference in the diameters between the donut box and the donut hole?

   A. 1 cm   C. 5 cm
   B. 3 cm   D. 8 cm

   7.G.4

DAY 6 *Challenge question*

Using the 4 circles from #s 1-2 on this page, what is the total area of those 4 circles? Leave your answer in terms of π.

7.G.4

118

Sometimes people only look at things from one angle. Not in Week 19! Here you can look at different kinds of angles like supplementary, complementary, adjacent and vertical angles. They are all special in their own ways – check them out!

**You can find detailed video explanations of each problem in the book by visiting:
ArgoPrep.com/ccm7**

WEEK 19 : DAY 1

1. Two angles are supplementary. The first angle measures 80° and the second angle is 2x. What is the value of x in degrees?

   A. 5°
   B. 10°
   C. 50°
   D. 100°

   7.G.5

The figure below is not to scale but should be used to answer questions 2 – 4. It is only shown to provide a visual of the relationship the angles have to each other.

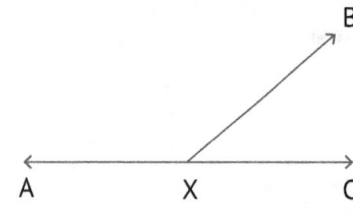

2. Angle AXC is 180°. If Angle AXB is 113°, what is the measure of Angle BXC?

   A. 57°
   B. 67°
   C. 193°
   D. 293°

   7.G.5

3. Angle AXC is 180°. If Angle AXB is 132°, what is the measure of Angle BXC?

   A. 48°
   B. 58°
   C. 128°
   D. 138°

   7.G.5

4. Angle AXC is 180°. If Angle CXB is 66°, what is the measure of Angle AXB?

   A. 24°
   B. 34°
   C. 104°
   D. 114°

   7.G.5

5. Line DE intersects Line FG at Point H as shown below. What is the measure of Angle DHF?

   A. 6°
   B. 20°
   C. 54°
   D. 87°

   Diagram: lines DE and FG intersect at H with angles $(5x - 13)°$ and $(4x + 7)°$.

   7.G.5

TIP of the DAY

Two angles that have a sum of 180° are called supplementary angles.

WEEK 19 : DAY 2

Use the figure below to answer questions 1 – 3.
The diagram is not to scale and is only to be used as an aid to understanding an angle's relationship to other angles in the diagram.
Angle SXV forms a straight angle and Angle UXR is also a straight angle. Angle RXS and Angle UXV are vertical angles.

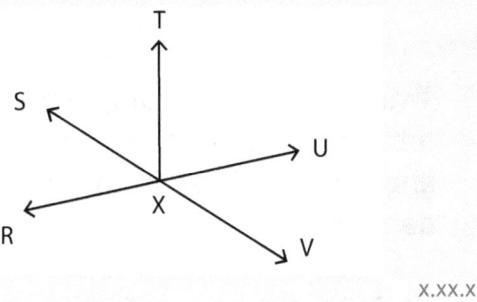

x.xx.x

1. If Angle SXR measures 49°, what is the measure of Angle UXV?

   A. 41°
   B. 49°
   C. 79°
   D. 131°

   7.G.5

2. If Angle SXR measures 49°, what is the measure of Angle RXV?

   A. 41°
   B. 49°
   C. 79°
   D. 131°

   7.G.5

3. If Angle RXV measures 129°, and Angle TXS measures 44°, what is the measure of Angle TXU?

   A. 44°
   B. 46°
   C. 85°
   D. 129°

   7.G.5

4. An isosceles triangle is shown below. What is the measure of Angle H?

   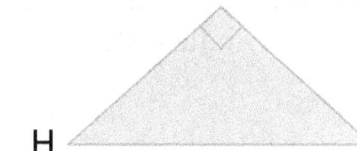

   A. 45°
   B. 90°
   C. 135°
   D. 180°

   7.G.5

5. If a cube is sliced with a plane that is perpendicular to its base, what shape is formed by the intersection of the cube and the plane?

   A. triangle
   B. pentagon
   C. rectangle
   D. square

   7.G.3

TIP of the DAY

Two angles that have a sum of 90° are called complementary angles.

121

WEEK 19 : DAY 3

The figure below is not to scale but should be used to answer questions 1 – 3. It is only shown to provide a visual of the relationship the angles have to each other.

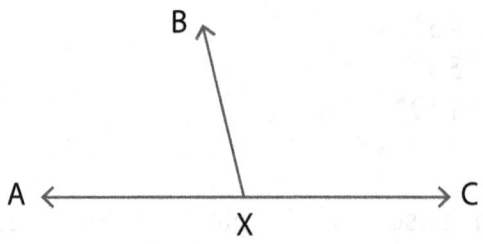

1. Angle AXC is 180°. If Angle AXB is 78°, what is the measure of Angle BXC?

   A. 12°
   B. 102°
   C. 112°
   D. 158°

   7.G.5

2. Angle AXC is 180°. If Angle BXC is 97°, what is the measure of Angle AXB?

   A. 83°
   B. 87°
   C. 93°
   D. 97°

   7.G.5

3. Angle AXC is 180°. If Angle CXB is 104°, what is the measure of Angle AXB?

   A. 14°
   B. 66°
   C. 76°
   D. 104°

   7.G.5

4. Two angles are complementary. The first angle measures 39° and the second angle is 3y. What is the value of y in degrees?

   A. 11°
   B. 17°
   C. 47°
   D. 51°

   7.G.5

5. Below is a picture of a sphere being sliced by a plane. What two-dimensional shape does this slice create?

   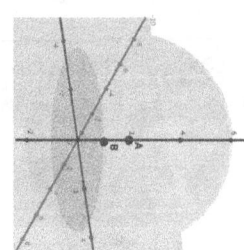

   A. square
   B. circle
   C. triangle
   D. oval

   7.G.3

TIP of the DAY: Vertical, or opposite, angles are equal. Two lines that intersect create vertical angles.

122

WEEK 19 : DAY 4

Use the figure below to answer questions 1 – 3. The diagram is not to scale and is only to be used as an aid to understanding an angle's relationship to other angles in the diagram. Line TU is intersected by Line RS at V.

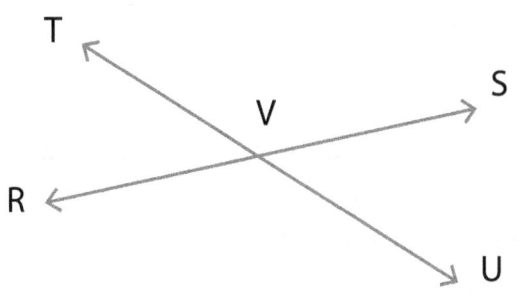

1. What type of angles are Angle RVT and Angle TVS?

   A. complementary
   B. opposite
   C. supplementary
   D. vertical

   7.G.5

2. If Angle SVU measures 63°, what is the measure of Angle SVT?

   A. 63°
   B. 93°
   C. 117°
   D. 147°

   7.G.5

3. If Angle RVT measures 55°, what is the measure of Angle SVU?

   A. 35°   C. 75°
   B. 55°   D. 125°

   7.G.5

4. The cone below is being sliced by a vertical plane that goes through the cone's endpoint. What two-dimensional shape is created at the intersection of the cone and the plane?

   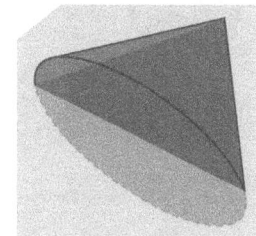

   A. triangle
   B. rectangle
   C. circle
   D. quadrilateral

   7.G.3

5. Harrison is kicking rocks into a bucket. The probability that he will kick a rock into the bucket is $\frac{5}{6}$. Which statement describes the probability that Harrison will get a rock into the bucket?

   A. likely   C. unlikely
   B. certain   D. impossible

   7.SP.5

TIP of the DAY

Adjacent angles are angles that share a common ray and common vertex. Adjacent angles do not overlap.

123

WEEK 19 : DAY 5

ASSESSMENT

1. Two angles are complementary. The first angle measures 42° and the second angle is 2x. What is the value of x in degrees?

   A. 24°
   B. 48°
   C. 69°
   D. 138°

   7.G.5

The figure below is not to scale but should be used to answer questions 2 – 3. It is only shown to provide a visual of the relationship the angles have to each other.

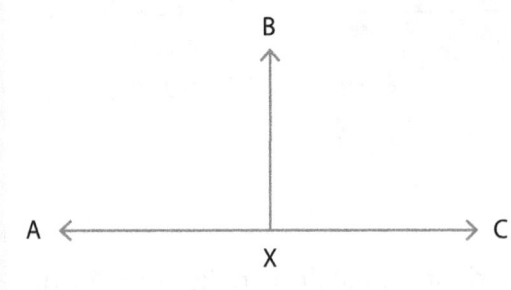

2. Angle AXC is 180°. If Angle AXB is 90°, what is the measure of Angle BXC?

   A. 45°
   B. 90°
   C. 135°
   D. 180°

   7.G.5

3. Angle AXB and Angle BXC are supplementary angles. If Angle AXB is an acute angle, which of the following measures could Angle BXC be?

   A. 1°
   B. 45°
   C. 88°
   D. 91°

   7.G.5

4. Angle K and Angle L are complementary angles. If Angle K is 17°, what is the measure of Angle L?

   A. 73°
   B. 83°
   C. 153°
   D. 163°

   7.G.5

5. On the figure below, Angle ACD is a straight line. If Angle DCB measures 132 degrees, what is the measure of Angle BCA?

   A. 48°
   B. 66°
   C. 76°
   D. 132°

   7.G.5

DAY 6 *Challenge question*

Angle A is 61° and Angle B is 61° as shown below. What are the measures of Angles ACB and BCD?

7.G.5

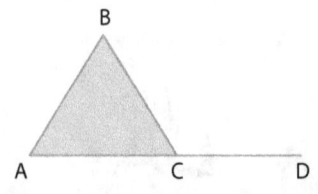

124

WEEK 20

VIDEO EXPLANATIONS
ARGOPREP.COM

You have done a great job making it this far! Let's finish the workbook by finding the volume, surface area and area of two- and three-dimensional objects. You may need to "break them down" into smaller triangles, rectangles, squares or other quadrilaterals.

**You can find detailed video explanations of each problem in the book by visiting:
ArgoPrep.com/ccm7**

WEEK 20 : DAY 1

Use the figure below to answer questions 1 – 2.

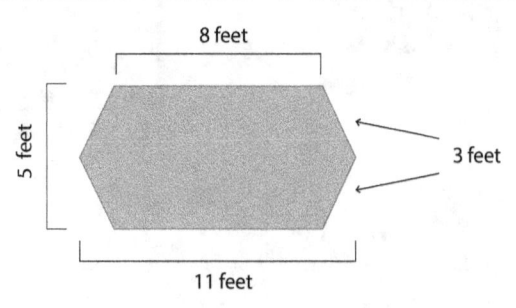

1. To find the area of the above figure, which area formulas could you NOT use?

   A. Area of a rectangle + (Area of a triangle × 2)
   B. Area of a trapezoid × 2
   C. Area of a rectangle + Area of a triangle + Area of a triangle
   D. Area of a square + Area of a triangle + Area of a trapezoid

   7.G.6

2. The dance teacher has 1 dance mat like the one above but he needs 1 more. How much material will he need to make 1 more mat like the one above?

   A. 44.5 feet³   C. 55.5 feet³
   B. 47.5 feet³   D. 94.5 feet³

   7.G.6

3. To play the ancient Viking game of Kubb, you need 10 pieces of wood like the one shown below. What is the total amount of wood required to play?

   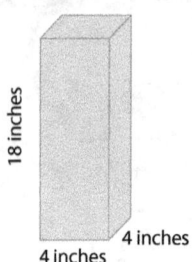

   A. 144 in³
   B. 288 in³
   C. 1,440 in³
   D. 2,880 in³

   7.G.6

4. A triangle has a base of 14 feet and a height of 17 feet. If 6 of these triangles were put together to form a hexagon, what would be the area of the hexagon?

   A. 119 ft²   C. 714 ft²
   B. 238 ft²   D. 1,428 ft²

   7.G.6

5. Line DE intersects Line FG at Point H as shown below. What is the measure of Angle DHG?

   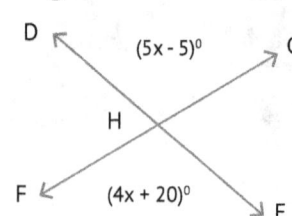

   A. 25°
   B. 60°
   C. 100°
   D. 120°

   7.G.5

TIP of the DAY

The volume of an object is the amount of space that it occupies.

WEEK 20 : DAY 2

Use the figure below to answer questions 1 – 4.

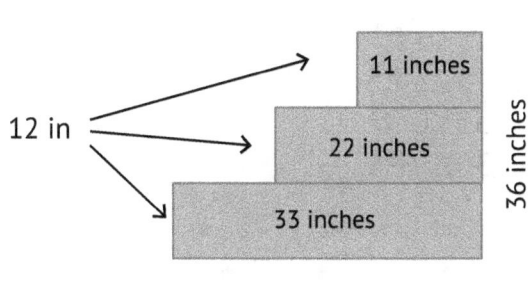

1. What is the total area of the stairs shown above?

   A. 132 in²
   B. 264 in²
   C. 402 in²
   D. 792 in²

2. The stairs shown above are **3 feet** wide. What is the volume of the stairs?

   A. 1,206 in³
   B. 2,376 in³
   C. 14,472 in³
   D. 28,512 in³

3. What is the total amount of surface area that would need to be carpeted?

   A. 1,584 in²
   B. 3,708 in²
   C. 5,364 in²
   D. 9,072 in²

4. If the stairs were to be reupholstered with new carpeting, which equation could be used to find how much carpet would be needed? (Remember carpet is not needed underneath the stairs, only the parts of the stairs that are visible.)

   A. (12 × 36) + (792 × 2) + (36 × 36) + (11 × 36)
   B. 3 (12 × 36) + (792 × 2) + (36 × 36) + 3 (11 × 36)
   C. 3 (12 × 36) + (792 × 2) + (36 × 36) + (11 × 36)
   D. (12 × 36) + (792 × 2) + (36 × 36) + 3 (11 × 36)

5. Yolanda randomly picked 10% of the 7th graders to ask them their favorite candy. If 42 of the students said MegaSugarBar, what is the most reasonable prediction of the number of 7th grade students who would pick MegaSugarBar as their favorite candy?

   A. 210
   B. 420
   C. 630
   D. 840

6. Vern is subtracting 22 from 31. Which equation could be used to find the difference between 31 and 22?

   A. 22 − 31
   B. 22 + (− 31)
   C. 31 + (− 22)
   D. − 31 + (− 22)

TIP of the DAY

Area is measured in square units (cm², in², ft²).

WEEK 20 : DAY 3

1. If each box is 1,024 cm³ in volume, how many complete boxes would fit into a box that is 180 cm × 200 cm × 12 cm?

   A. 124
   B. 257
   C. 374
   D. 421

   7.G.6

William is making a tent like the one shown below. **Use the drawing of the tent to answer questions 2 – 3.**

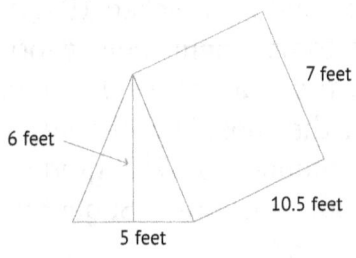

2. If William does not need material for the floor, how much material will he need to make the tent?

   A. 177 ft²
   B. 207 ft²
   C. 229.5 ft²
   D. 237 ft²

   7.G.6

3. How much space will William's tent occupy after he sets it up?

   A. 157.5 ft³
   B. 183.8 ft³
   C. 315.0 ft³
   D. 367.5 ft³

   7.G.6

4. Which equation could NOT be used to solve for the missing angle below?

   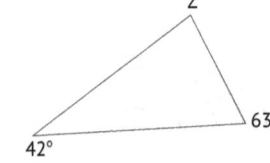

   A. $42 + 63 = Z - 180$
   B. $Z = 180 - 42 - 63$
   C. $Z + 42 + 63 = 180$
   D. $180 - Z = 42 + 63$

   7.G.5

5. Line DE intersects Line FG at Point H as shown below. What is the value of x?

   A. 22°
   B. 44°
   C. 66°
   D. 88°

   7.G.5

TIP of the DAY

When finding the area of triangles and trapezoids, remember to divide by 2.

128

WEEK 20 : DAY 4

There are 4 circles shown below. **Use and the diagram to answer questions 1 – 2.** Answer choices may have been rounded.

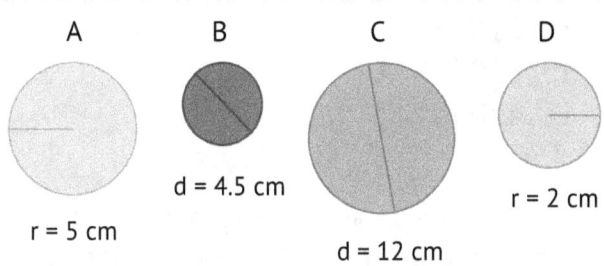

1. What is the circumference of Circle A?

    A. 15.7 cm
    B. 31.4 cm
    C. 78.5 cm
    D. 314 cm

    7.G.4

2. What is the area of Circle D?

    A. 12.56 cm²
    B. 15.7 cm²
    C. 25.12 cm²
    D. 32.48 cm²

    7.G.4

3. There is a gift that Vanessa has. It is 8 inches by 5 inches by 6 inches. What is the volume of the gift?

    A. 180 in³
    B. 190 in³
    C. 210 in³
    D. 240 in³

    7.G.6

4. Vanessa wants to wrap the gift she has. EXACTLY how much wrapping paper will Vanessa need to wrap the gift (with no overlap)?

    A. 118 in²
    B. 194 in²
    C. 236 in²
    D. 262 in²

    7.G.6

5. The car was priced at $18,519. The dealer discounted it by 19% during the "Car Sell-a-bration". The next week they increased the price by 2%. What is the price now?

    A. $15,000.39
    B. $15,300.40
    C. $15,370.77
    D. $15,412.50

    7.RP.3

TIP of the DAY

Volume is measured in cubic units (mi³, m³, km³) because 3 dimensions are used – length, width and depth.

129

WEEK 20 : DAY 5

ASSESSMENT

1. If a unit cube is 1 mm³ in volume, how many complete unit cubes would fit into a box that is 320 mm × 158 mm × 15 mm?

   A. 75,840
   B. 758,400
   C. 7,584,000
   D. 75,840,000

   7.G.6

3. If the figure shown were 5 inches thick, what would be its volume?

   A. 105 in³
   B. 210 in³
   C. 330 in³
   D. 420 in³

   7.G.6

Use the figure below to answer questions 2 – 3.

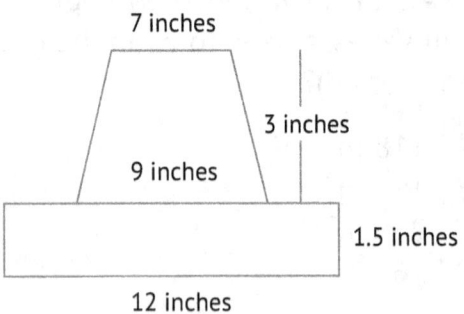

Below is a game board where players are to "call" a number and/or a color. If the quarter lands on a square that the player "called," they win a point. **Use the picture below to answer questions 4 – 5.**

| 1 | 3 | 5 | 7 |
| 2 | 4 | 6 | 8 |

2. What is the area of the figure shown above?

   A. 42 in²
   B. 66 in²
   C. 84 in²
   D. 170 in²

   7.G.6

4. What is the probability that a player would land on a white square?

   A. $\frac{1}{8}$ C. $\frac{1}{4}$
   B. $\frac{3}{8}$ D. $\frac{1}{2}$

   7.SP.6

DAY 6
Challenge question

What are some ways you can "break apart" this hexagon to find its area?

7.G.6

130

Great job finishing all 20 weeks! You should be ready for any test.

ASSESSMENT

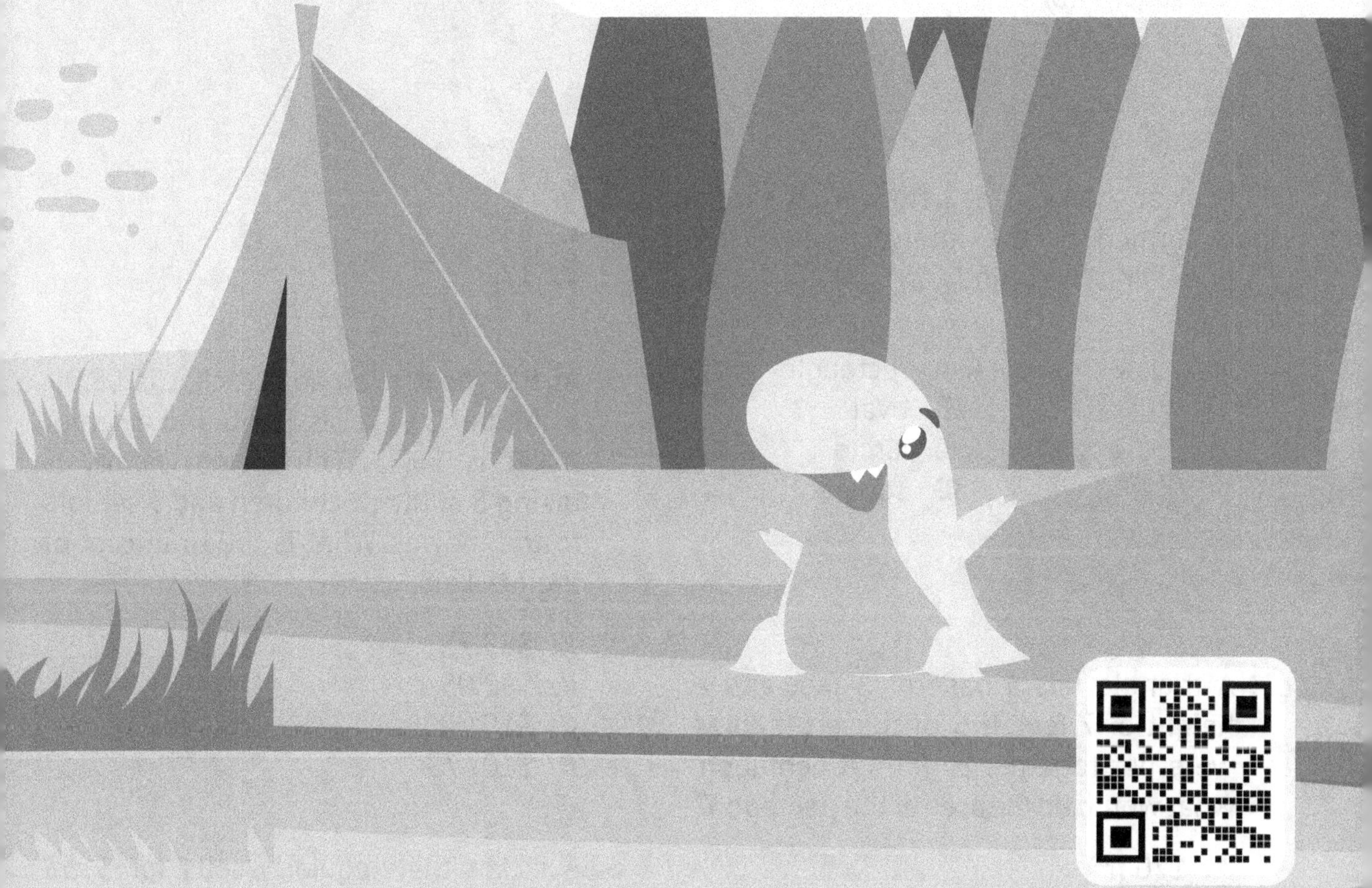

Try this assessment to see how much you've learned - good luck!

ASSESSMENT

1. Which expression represents a factorization of 15ab + 12b?

   A. 3b (5a + 4)
   B. 3b (5a + 4b)
   C. 3b (5 + 4b)
   D. 3ab (5 + 4)

   7.EE.1

2. Look at the cylinder below. What shape is formed by the intersection of the plane and the cylinder?

   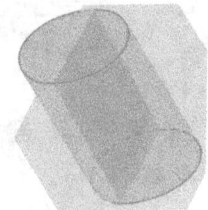

   A. rectangle
   B. oval
   C. circle
   D. square

   7.G.3

3. A triangle has a base of 8 feet and a height of 7 feet. If 5 of these triangles were put together to form a pentagon, what would be the area of the pentagon?

   A. 120 ft²
   B. 140 ft²
   C. 240 ft²
   D. 280 ft²

   7.G.6

4. Use the figure below where Angle AXC is 180°. If Angle AXB is 127°, what is the measure of Angle BXC?

   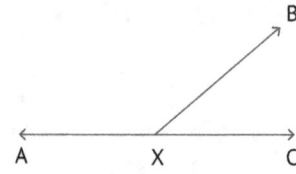

   A. 37°
   B. 53°
   C. 63°
   D. 127

   7.G.5

5. At the theatre, an adult ticket is $8.95, a children's ticket is $4.50 and a senior ticket is $6.75. The Snyder family is taking 5 adults, 8 children and 3 seniors to the movies. What is the total cost of their tickets?

   A. $89.75
   B. $92.05
   C. $101.00
   D. $107.75

   7.NS.3

6. A jacket that regularly sells for $153 was on sale for 40% off the regular price. What is the sale price?

   A. $61.20
   B. $79.40
   C. $91.80
   D. $113.00

   7.EE.3

134

ASSESSMENT

7. Ada has a box of toys. The probability that she will randomly pick out a princess toy is $\frac{1}{5}$. Which statement describes the probability that Ada will pick a princess toy?

   A. likely
   B. certain
   C. unlikely
   D. impossible

   7.SP.5

8. Potatoes cost $1.35 per pound. What equation is used to find C, the total cost for p pounds of potatoes?

   A. $C = 1.35p$
   B. $C = 1.35 + p$
   C. $C + 1.35 = p$
   D. $1.35C = p$

   7.RP.2

Zeke's scores are shown below.
Use the information to answer questions 9 – 10.
French: 71, 70, 85, 94, 79, 89, 91
Biology: 94, 80, 92, 86, 82, 97, 87

9. What is the approximate difference between the ranges of Zeke's 2 class scores?

   A. 3
   B. 5
   C. 6
   D. 7

   7.SP.3

10. Which statement is true about Zeke's French and biology scores?

    A. Zeke's biology scores had a larger range.
    B. Zeke's median score for French was larger than his median score for biology.
    C. Zeke's mean score for biology was smaller than his mean score for French.
    D. Zeke's median score for biology was larger than his mean score for French.

    7.SP.3

11. If 25% of players are surveyed and 36 of them say they prefer to play defense, what is the most reasonable prediction of the number of players who would prefer to play defense?

    A. 61
    B. 144
    C. 180
    D. 215

    7.SP.2

135

ASSESSMENT

12. There is a triangle that has 2 angles that measure 100° and 21°. What is the measure of the third angle?

    A. 59°
    B. 79°
    C. 121°
    D. 180°

    7.G.2

13. Two angles are complementary. The first angle measures 15° and the second angle is 3y. What is the value of y in degrees?

    A. 25°
    B. 55°
    C. 75°
    D. 165°

    7.G.5

14. The mean radius of Egg Harbor Park is 12 miles and the mean radius of Green Park is 5 miles. What is the approximate difference in the mean circumferences, in miles, of the 2 parks? Round your answer to the nearest tenth of a mile.

    A. 10.86 miles
    B. 17.14 miles
    C. 21.98 miles
    D. 43.96 miles

    7.G.4

15. Zorah bought a pair of shoes that were discounted $12\frac{1}{2}$ %. If the non-sale price was s, which expression represents the cost Zorah paid for the shoes?

    A. 1 - 0.125
    B. 1 - 0.125s
    C. 0.875s
    D. s - 0.875

    7.EE.2

16. Nelson wants to purchase a rowboat for $698. Each month he is able to save $57 for the purchase. If he has $192 already set aside, how many months will it take Nelson to save enough money to buy the rowboat?

    A. 8
    B. 9
    C. 10
    D. 11

    7.EE.4

17. Mason's driving test score was a 36. After he retook the driving test, his score was 45. What is the percent increase from the first test to the second test?

    A. 20%
    B. 25%
    C. 28%
    D. 33%

    7.RP.3

ASSESSMENT

18. What is the product of $\left(\frac{4}{12}\right) \times \left(-\frac{5}{3}\right)$?

A. $\frac{-5}{9}$

B. $\frac{5}{9}$

C. $\frac{-1}{5}$

D. $\frac{1}{5}$

7.NS.2

19. The grocery store wants to know which type of meat is the most popular at its store. Which population would be the best group to ask?

A. Vegetarians who shop at the store
B. Every 10th person who enters the meat section
C. Half of the people who purchase cheese at the deli
D. Every 6th person who is in the milk and egg aisle

7.SP.1

20. If the probability of Latina drawing a purple shirt from the laundry is $\frac{3}{8}$ and she randomly draws 1 shirt at a time and replaces it, how many times would you expect Latina to get a purple shirt if she tries 152 times?

A. 19
B. 38
C. 57
D. 83

7.SP.1

21. The probability that Boone will score a goal is $\frac{1}{5}$. The probability that Keeley will score a goal is $\frac{1}{4}$. What is the probability that both Boone and Keeley will score?

A. $\frac{1}{1}$

B. $\frac{1}{9}$

C. $\frac{1}{19}$

D. $\frac{1}{20}$

7.SP.8

22. Dell was able to plant $3\frac{2}{3}$ rows of watermelon in 15 minutes. How many rows could Dell plant in an hour?

A. $11\frac{1}{3}$

B. $14\frac{2}{3}$

C. $18\frac{2}{3}$

D. $21\frac{1}{3}$

7.RP.1

23. Mr. Wiggins has 35 dollars and he earns 12 dollars for every piano lesson he teaches. Which equation shows how many dollars, D, that Mr. Wiggins has after L lessons?

A. $D = 12L + 35$
B. $D = 12L - 35$
C. $D = 35L + 12$
D. $D = 47L$

7.EE.4

137

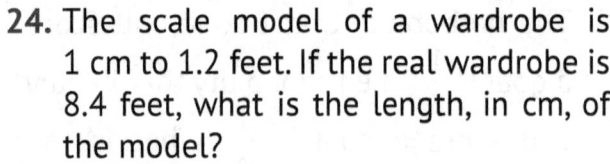

24. The scale model of a wardrobe is 1 cm to 1.2 feet. If the real wardrobe is 8.4 feet, what is the length, in cm, of the model?

   A. 7.0 cm
   B. 7.2 cm
   C. 8.4 cm
   D. 9.6 cm

   7.G.1

25. Below are some measurements that were taken by a fisherman. He measured 2 types of fish and charted the information. Use the table below to answer the question.

Number	Pike (pounds)	Salmon (pounds)
1	25	35
2	18	22
3	27	28
4	23	24

Which statement is NOT true about the fish that were measured?

   A. The salmon tended to weigh more than the pike.
   B. The pike weights had a larger range than the salmon weights.
   C. The salmon's mean weight is 4 pounds larger than the pike's mean weight.
   D. The median of the pike is less than the median of the salmon.

   7.SP.4

26. Which property is shown below?

   $(3x + y) + 4z = 3x + (y + 4z)$

   A. Associative Property
   B. Commutative Property
   C. Distributive Property
   D. Inverse Property

   7.EE.1

27. The circumference of a circle is 25π cm. What is the area, in square cm, of the circle? Express your answer in terms of π.

   _____

   7.G.4

28. Convert $\frac{8}{3}$ to its decimal equivalent using long division.

   _____

   7.NS.2

138

ASSESSMENT

There are 50 tokens in a box and the number of each color is shown below. **Use the table below to answer questions 29 - 30.**

Color	Number
Yellow	12
Purple	10
Green	8
Red	11
Black	9

29. Based on the data, what is the probability that Bay will draw out a red token?

_____

7.SP.7

30. Based on the data, what is the probability that Zak will draw out a green token?

_____

7.SP.7

31. Trace earns $10.70 for the first 11 hours he works and $11.45 for every hour after that. If Trace worked $20\frac{1}{2}$ hours, how much would he earn?

_____

7.EE.3

32. Four girls bought some beads to share. Each pound of beads was $1.78 each. They bought 8 pounds of beads. If they also shared the price, how much money would each girl contribute?

_____

7.NS.3

33. Below are some transactions (in dollars) that Beatrix made with her bank account.

Deposits	Withdrawals
91.78	- 153.17
432.50	- 460.85

If Beatrix's account had $145 before any deposits or withdrawals, what was her final balance?

_____

7.NS.1

ASSESSMENT

34. There are 2 six-sided fair dice. How many possible outcomes are there if both dice are thrown at the same time?

_____

7.SP.7

35. Waylon is spinning a spinner. The probability that the spinner will land on 4 on his next turn is $\frac{1}{7}$. Which word could be used to describe the probability that Waylon's next spin will be a 4?

_____

7.SP.5

36. What is the constant of proportionality for the table below?

x	y
8	4
10	5
7	3.5

_____

7.RP.2

37. Stella ran $15\frac{2}{5}$ km in 2 hours. How far could Stella run in 5 hours?

_____

7.RP.1

38. There is a right triangle that has a side that is 55°. How many degrees is the third angle?

_____

7.G.2

39. You are to solve the equation:

$$-12d = 16$$

What step should you take first?

_____

7.EE.4

140

ASSESSMENT

40. There were 1500 pairs of headphones in stock on Friday. The number of headphones went down 20% after the weekend. On Wednesday, 10% more stock was added. How many headphones are in stock now?

_____

7.RP.3

41. The diagram below shows the dimensions of a dining room. If a scale model were built so that 3 centimeters on the model represented 2 feet of the actual room, what would be the length, in centimeters, of the model?

Length: 10 feet
Width: 8 feet

_____

7.G.1

42. Below is a model made up of a square and a triangle. What is the area of the model?

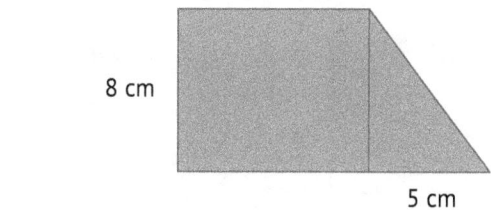
8 cm
5 cm

_____

7.G.6

43. Altitude above sea level is given in positive values and below sea level is given in negative values. If Yancey started at 1,287 meters above sea level and decreased his altitude by 4,165 meters before increasing his altitude by 2,039 meters, what was his final altitude?

_____

7.NS.1

141

ANSWER KEY

VIDEO EXPLANATIONS

ANSWER KEY

WEEK 1

DAY 1	DAY 2	DAY 3	DAY 4	DAY 5
1. B	1. C	1. B	1. A	1. A
2. B	2. B	2. C	2. B	2. A
3. B	3. D	3. D	3. B	3. B
4. D	4. A	4. C	4. C	4. C
5. B	5. B	5. D	5. D	5. D
		6. A	6. C	

WEEK 2

DAY 1	DAY 2	DAY 3	DAY 4	DAY 5
1. B	1. C	1. B	1. B	1. C
2. C	2. A	2. C	2. A	2. B
3. B	3. A	3. B	3. D	3. A
4. D	4. B	4. D	4. B	4. B
5. A	5. C	5. A	5. B	5. C
6. D	6. D	6. B	6. A	6. C

WEEK 3

DAY 1	DAY 2	DAY 3	DAY 4	DAY 5
1. A	1. B	1. C	1. D	1. A
2. A	2. B	2. B	2. C	2. C
3. D	3. D	3. C	3. B	3. B
4. C	4. C	4. C	4. A	4. C
5. A	5. A	5. D	5. C	5. D
6. A			6. C	

WEEK 4

DAY 1	DAY 2	DAY 3	DAY 4	DAY 5
1. D	1. B	1. C	1. A	1. D
2. C	2. C	2. B	2. C	2. A
3. A	3. A	3. A	3. C	3. C
4. D	4. D	4. D	4. C	4. B
5. D	5. D	5. C	5. B	5. D
6. B				

WEEK 5

DAY 1	DAY 2	DAY 3	DAY 4	DAY 5
1. B	1. D	1. C	1. C	1. A
2. B	2. C	2. B	2. B	2. A
3. B	3. B	3. B	3. B	3. D
4. A	4. B	4. D	4. B	4. D
5. A	5. A	5. B		5. C
6. C				

WEEK 6

DAY 1	DAY 2	DAY 3	DAY 4	DAY 5
1. A	1. D	1. B	1. A	1. B
2. B	2. C	2. A	2. D	2. B
3. C	3. A	3. B	3. B	3. A
4. B	4. A	4. A	4. A	4. C
5. D	5. B	5. D	5. D	5. A
6. A	6. C	6. B		

ANSWER KEY

WEEK 7

DAY 1	DAY 2	DAY 3	DAY 4	DAY 5
1. C	1. B	1. D	1. D	1. A
2. D	2. C	2. A	2. B	2. D
3. D	3. A	3. D	3. C	3. A
4. C	4. D	4. A	4. B	4. A
5. C	5. B	5. B	5. B	5. C
6. A	6. D			

WEEK 8

DAY 1	DAY 2	DAY 3	DAY 4	DAY 5
1. B	1. B	1. D	1. B	1. C
2. C	2. C	2. C	2. C	2. D
3. A	3. B	3. C	3. B	3. D
4. B	4. C	4. A	4. D	4. D
5. C	5. A	5. D	5. A	5. B
6. D	6. B		6. D	

WEEK 9

DAY 1	DAY 2	DAY 3	DAY 4	DAY 5
1. B	1. B	1. D	1. D	1. C
2. A	2. C	2. C	2. C	2. C
3. D	3. D	3. D	3. C	3. D
4. A	4. C	4. B	4. D	4. A
				5. C

WEEK 10

DAY 1	DAY 2	DAY 3	DAY 4	DAY 5
1. A	1. A	1. C	1. B	1. A
2. B	2. D	2. A	2. B	2. B
3. A	3. B	3. B	3. D	3. A
4. B	4. C	4. A	4. C	4. C
			5. B	5. C
			6. C	6. C

WEEK 11

DAY 1	DAY 2	DAY 3	DAY 4	DAY 5
1. B	1. B	1. C	1. A	1. D
2. C	2. C	2. D	2. C	2. B
3. A	3. B	3. A	3. A	3. A
4. C	4. A	4. A	4. A	4. C
5. B	5. B	5. B	5. A	
	6. A			

WEEK 12

DAY 1	DAY 2	DAY 3	DAY 4	DAY 5
1. C	1. A	1. A	1. B	1. C
2. C	2. B	2. C	2. D	2. D
3. B	3. C	3. C	3. A	3. A
4. D	4. D	4. B	4. B	4. A
5. A	5. A	5. C	5. A	5. B
6. A	6. B		6. A	

ANSWER KEY

WEEK 13

DAY 1	DAY 2	DAY 3	DAY 4	DAY 5
1. C	1. D	1. B	1. C	1. B
2. A	2. A	2. C	2. B	2. A
3. B	3. A	3. D	3. D	3. C
4. C	4. A	4. C	4. A	4. B
5. D	5. B	5. B	5. B	

WEEK 14

DAY 1	DAY 2	DAY 3	DAY 4	DAY 5
1. D	1. D	1. B	1. C	1. D
2. D	2. B	2. D	2. D	2. C
3. D	3. A	3. C	3. C	3. D
4. A	4. A	4. C	4. C	4. C
5. A	5. C	5. D	5. A	5. D
		6. C		

WEEK 15

DAY 1	DAY 2	DAY 3	DAY 4	DAY 5
1. C	1. B	1. C	1. A	1. B
2. D	2. B	2. A	2. B	2. A
3. B	3. D	3. C	3. B	3. D
4. C	4. C	4. A	4. C	4. C
5. D	5. A	5. B	5. B	5. B
6. B		6. D	6. A	6. B

WEEK 16

DAY 1	DAY 2	DAY 3	DAY 4	DAY 5
1. A	1. A	1. C	1. B	1. D
2. C	2. C	2. D	2. D	2. A
3. B	3. B	3. A	3. C	3. B
4. A	4. D	4. A	4. A	4. B
5. A	5. C	5. D	5. B	5. C
	6. D		6. C	

WEEK 17

DAY 1	DAY 2	DAY 3	DAY 4	DAY 5
1. A	1. A	1. D	1. A	1. A
2. C	2. C	2. A	2. D	2. A
3. D	3. D	3. C	3. B	3. C
4. B	4. A	4. D	4. C	4. A
5. B	5. B	5. B	5. D	5. B
6. D	6. C	6. D	6. C	6. B

WEEK 18

DAY 1	DAY 2	DAY 3	DAY 4	DAY 5
1. C	1. B	1. A	1. B	1. A
2. A	2. D	2. C	2. A	2. B
3. C	3. C	3. D	3. C	3. D
4. B	4. A	4. A	4. D	4. C
5. D	5. C	5. A	5. C	5. C
	6. B			

ANSWER KEY

WEEK 19

DAY 1	DAY 2	DAY 3	DAY 4	DAY 5
1. C	1. B	1. B	1. C	1. A
2. B	2. D	2. A	2. C	2. B
3. A	3. C	3. C	3. B	3. D
4. D	4. A	4. B	4. A	4. A
5. D	5. D	5. B	5. A	5. A

WEEK 20

DAY 1	DAY 2	DAY 3	DAY 4	DAY 5
1. D	1. D	1. D	1. B	1. B
2. B	2. D	2. A	2. A	2. A
3. D	3. C	3. A	3. D	3. B
4. C	4. B	4. A	4. C	4. B
5. D	5. B	5. A	5. B	5. B
	6. C			

CHALLENGE QUESTIONS

WEEK 1
-4.5°C

WEEK 2
$1,656

WEEK 3
$9a(4 - 2b + 3c)$

WEEK 4
$p - 0.15p$ or $0.85p$

WEEK 5
$19\frac{5}{24}$ feet

WEEK 6
$G = 8.95w - 25$

WEEK 7
4

WEEK 8
Hyatt increased by 12.5% and Jensen increased by 4.5%. Hyatt had the larger percent of increase.

WEEK 9
880

WEEK 10
140 players hit home runs

WEEK 11
$\frac{3}{8}$ inch

WEEK 12
$\frac{1}{8}$ or 0.125

WEEK 13
$\frac{1}{36}$

WEEK 14
$\frac{1}{172,800}$

WEEK 15
7.5 m × 10.5 m

WEEK 16
73

WEEK 17
decagon

WEEK 18
114.5π yards^2

WEEK 19
Angle ACB is 58° and Angle BCD is 122°

WEEK 20
It can broken into either: 6 triangles, 2 trapezoids, 1 rectangle + 2 triangles OR 2 rectangles + 2 (or 4) triangles.

ANSWER KEY Assessment

1. A
2. A
3. B
4. B
5. C
6. C
7. C
8. A
9. D
10. D
11. B
12. A
13. A
14. D
15. C
16. B
17. B
18. A
19. B
20. C
21. D
22. B
23. A
24. A
25. B
26. A
27. 156.25 πcm²
28. 2.666....
29. $\frac{11}{50}$
30. $\frac{4}{25}$
31. $226.48
32. $3.56
33. $55.26
34. 36
35. unlikely
36. $\frac{1}{2}$
37. 38.5 km
38. 35°
39. Divide by − 12 or multiply by − $\frac{1}{12}$
40. 1,320 headphones
41. 15 cm
42. 84 cm²
43. - 839 meters

SOCIAL STUDIES

Social Studies Daily Practice Workbook by ArgoPrep allows students to build foundational skills and review concepts. Our workbooks explore social studies topics in depth with ArgoPrep's 5 E's to build social studies mastery.

KIDS WINTER ACADEMY

Kids Winter Academy by ArgoPrep covers material learned in September through December so your child can reinforce the concepts they should have learned in class. We recommend using this particular series during the winter break. These workbooks include two weeks of activities for math, reading, science, and social studies. Best of all, you can access detailed video explanations to all the questions on our website.

DIPLOMA

The certificate is presented to:

_____
your name

_____
by school name

for successful completion of ArgoPrep's Grade 7 workbook

_____
Date

_____
Signature

7th Grade

Excellent work!

argoprep.com

www.ingramcontent.com/pod-product-compliance
Lightning Source LLC
Chambersburg PA
CBHW051804100526
44592CB00016B/2559